# LEVEL 3 Supplemental
## ANSWER BOOK

By Glory St. Germain ARCT RMT MYCC UMTC &
Shelagh McKibbon-U'Ren RMT UMTC

The LEVEL 3 Supplemental Workbook is designed to be completed after the Prep 2 Rudiments and Level 2 Supplemental Workbook.

# GSG MUSIC
*Enriching Lives Through Music Education*

ISBN: 978-1-927641-54-5

# The Ultimate Music Theory™ Program

The Ultimate Music Theory™ Program lays the foundation of music theory education.

The focus of the Ultimate Music Theory Program is to simplify complex concepts and show the relativity of these concepts with practical application. This program is designed to help teachers and students discover the excitement and benefits of a sound music theory education.

The Ultimate Music Theory Program is based on a proven approach to the study of music theory that follows the *"must have"* Learning Principles to develop effective learning for all learning styles.

The Ultimate Music Theory™ Program and Supplemental Workbooks help students prepare for nationally recognized theory examinations including the Royal Conservatory of Music.

# GSG MUSIC

Library and Archives Canada Cataloguing in Publication
UMT Supplemental Series / Glory St. Germain and Shelagh McKibbon-U'Ren

**Gloryland Publishing - UMT Supplemental Workbook and Answer Book Series:**

| | | |
|---|---|---|
| GP-SPL | ISBN: 978-1-927641-41-5 | UMT Supplemental Prep Level |
| GP-SL1 | ISBN: 978-1-927641-42-2 | UMT Supplemental Level 1 |
| GP-SL2 | ISBN: 978-1-927641-43-9 | UMT Supplemental Level 2 |
| GP-SL3 | ISBN: 978-1-927641-44-6 | UMT Supplemental Level 3 |
| GP-SL4 | ISBN: 978-1-927641-45-3 | UMT Supplemental Level 4 |
| GP-SL5 | ISBN: 978-1-927641-46-0 | UMT Supplemental Level 5 |
| GP-SL6 | ISBN: 978-1-927641-47-7 | UMT Supplemental Level 6 |
| GP-SL7 | ISBN: 978-1-927641-48-4 | UMT Supplemental Level 7 |
| GP-SL8 | ISBN: 978-1-927641-49-1 | UMT Supplemental Level 8 |
| GP-SCL | ISBN: 978-1-927641-50-7 | UMT Supplemental Complete Level |
| GP-SPLA | ISBN: 978-1-927641-51-4 | UMT Supplemental Prep Level Answer Book |
| GP-SL1A | ISBN: 978-1-927641-52-1 | UMT Supplemental Level 1 Answer Book |
| GP-SL2A | ISBN: 978-1-927641-53-8 | UMT Supplemental Level 2 Answer Book |
| GP-SL3A | ISBN: 978-1-927641-54-5 | UMT Supplemental Level 3 Answer Book |
| GP-SL4A | ISBN: 978-1-927641-55-2 | UMT Supplemental Level 4 Answer Book |
| GP-SL5A | ISBN: 978-1-927641-56-9 | UMT Supplemental Level 5 Answer Book |
| GP-SL6A | ISBN: 978-1-927641-57-6 | UMT Supplemental Level 6 Answer Book |
| GP-SL7A | ISBN: 978-1-927641-58-3 | UMT Supplemental Level 7 Answer Book |
| GP-SL8A | ISBN: 978-1-927641-59-0 | UMT Supplemental Level 8 Answer Book |
| GP-SCLA | ISBN: 978-1-927641-60-6 | UMT Supplemental Complete Level Answer Book |

**Respect Copyright** - Copyright 2017 Gloryland Publishing

All rights reserved. No part of this publication may be reproduced or transmitted in any form or by any means, electronic or mechanical, including photocopying, recording, or any information storage and retrieval system, without permission in writing from the author/publisher.

\* Resources - An annotated list is available at UltimateMusicTheory.com under Free Resources.

# Ultimate Music Theory

## LEVEL 3 Supplemental

### Table of Contents

| | | |
|---|---|---|
| **Ultimate Music Theory** | The Story of UMT… Meet So-La & Ti-Do | 4 |
| **Comparison Chart** | Level 3 | 6 |
| **Notes and Beams** | Eighth and Sixteenth | 8 |
| **Function of a Dot** | Dotted Notes and Dotted Rests | 10 |
| **Rhythm Review** | Adding Rests | 12 |
| **Time Signatures** | Upbeat (Anacrusis) and Adding Bar Lines | 14 |
| **Scale Degrees** | Major and Minor (natural) Scales | 16 |
| **Scale Degrees** | Minor (harmonic and melodic) Scales | 18 |
| **Intervals** | Perfect, Major and minor thirds | 20 |
| **Writing Intervals** | Using a Key Signature (Root is Tonic) | 22 |
| **Writing Intervals** | Using a Key Signature (Root is NOT Tonic) | 24 |
| **Writing Intervals** | Using Accidentals or a Key Signature | 26 |
| **Major and Minor Triads** | Tonic and Dominant (Major & Harmonic minor scales) | 28 |
| **Tonic and Dominant** | Functional Chord Symbols (Major & Harmonic minor scales) | 30 |
| **Major and Minor Keys** | Root/Quality Chord Symbols (Tonic and Dominant) | 32 |
| **Writing Chords** | Tonic and Dominant and Chord Chaos Game | 34 |
| **Terms & Transposition** | Style in Performance and Transposing One Octave | 36 |
| **Analysis and Melody** | Melodic Phrases and Leaps between Notes | 38 |
| **Melody Writing** | Scale degrees and Analysis - Motive and Phrases | 40 |
| **ICE & Analysis** | Imagine, Compose, Explore & Sight Reading - Little Hamster | 42 |
| **Music History** | Bach and the Anna Magdalena Notebook | 44 |
| **Music for Dancing** | Baroque Dances and the Harpsichord | 46 |
| **Listening Activity** | Petzold's Menuet in G Major, BWV Anh. 114 | 47 |
| **Listening Activity** | Bach's French Suite No. 5 in G Major, BWV 816 | 48 |
| **Theory Exam** | Level 3 | 50 |
| **Certificate** | Completion of Level 3 | 56 |

**Score: 60 - 69** Pass;  **70 - 79** Honors;  **80 - 89** First Class Honors;  **90 - 100** First Class Honors with Distinction

Ultimate Music Theory: *The Way to Score Success!*

**Workbooks, Exams, Answers, Online Courses, App & More!**

A Proven Step-by-Step System to Learn Theory Faster - from Beginner to Advanced.

Innovative techniques designed to develop a complete understanding of music theory, to enhance sight reading, ear training, creativity, composition and musical expression.

## All UMT Series have matching Answer Books!

**The UMT Rudiments Series - Beginner A, Beginner B, Beginner C, Prep 1, Prep 2, Basic, Intermediate, Advanced & Complete (All-In-One)**

♪ 12 Lessons, Review Tests, and a Final Exam to develop confidence
♪ Music Theory Guide & Chart for fast and easy reference of theory concepts
♪ 80 Flashcards for fun drills to dramatically increase retention & comprehension

**Rudiments Exam Series - Preparatory, Basic, Intermediate & Advanced**

♪ 8 Exams plus UMT Tips on How to Score 100% on Theory Exams

## Each Rudiments Workbook correlates to a Supplemental Workbook.

**The UMT Supplemental Series - Prep Level, Level 1, Level 2, Level 3, Level 4, Level 5, Level 6, Level 7, Level 8 & Complete (All-In-One) Level**

♪ Form & Analysis and Music History - Composers, Eras & Musical Styles
♪ Melody Writing using ICE - Imagine, Compose & Explore
♪ 12 Lessons, Review Tests, Final Exam and 80 Flashcards for quick study

**Supplemental Exam Series - Level 5, Level 6, Level 7 & Level 8**

♪ 8 Exams to successfully prepare for nationally recognized Theory Exams

**UMT Online Courses, Music Theory App & More**

♪ UMT Certification Course, Teachers Membership & Elite Educator Program
♪ Ultimate Music Theory App correlates to the Rudiments Workbooks
♪ Free Resources - Teachers Guide, Music Theory Blogs, videos & downloads

### Go To: UltimateMusicTheory.com

At Ultimate Music Theory we are passionate about helping teachers and students experience the joy of teaching and learning music by creating the most effective music theory materials on the planet!

**Introducing the Ultimate Music Theory Family!**

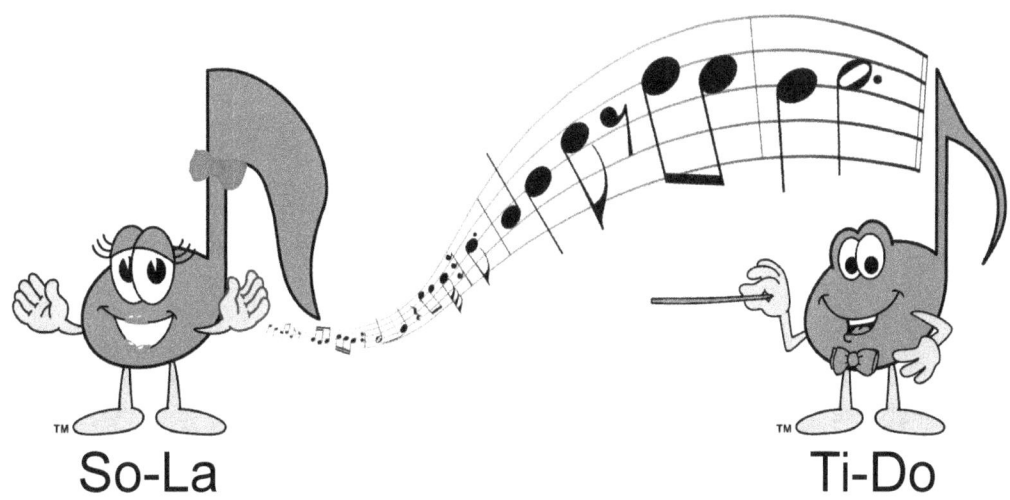

### So-La

Meet So-La! So-La loves to sing and dance.

She is expressive, creative and loves to tell stories through music!

So-La feels music in her heart. She loves to teach, compose and perform.

### Ti-Do

Meet Ti-Do! Ti-Do loves to count and march.

He is rhythmic, consistent and loves the rules of music theory!

Ti-Do feels music in his hands and feet. He loves to analyze, share tips and conduct.

So-La & Ti-Do will guide you through Mastering Music Theory!

*Enriching Lives Through Music Education*

# The Ultimate Music Theory™ Comparison Chart to the 2016 Royal Conservatory of Music Theory Syllabus.
## Level 3

The Ultimate Music Theory™ Rudiments Workbooks, Supplemental Workbooks and Exams prepare students for successful completion of the Royal Conservatory of Music Theory Levels.

UMT Prep 2 Rudiments Workbook plus the LEVEL 2 Supplemental = RCM Theory Level 2.
♫ Note: Additional completion of the LEVEL 3 Supplemental Workbook = RCM Theory Level 3.

| RCM Level 3 Theory Concept | Ultimate Music Theory Prep 2 Workbook |
|---|---|
| **Required Keys:**<br>- C, G, D, F, B-flat Major; a, e, b, d, g minor | **Keys Covered:**<br>- C, G, D, F, B-flat Major; a, e, b, d, g minor |
| **Pitch and Notation:**<br>- Enharmonic Equivalents<br><br>- Transposition up/down one octave | **Pitch and Notation Covered:**<br>- Whole Steps, Half Steps, Enharmonic Equivalents and Same pitch, different name<br>* Workbook Page - Melody Transposition - Up or Down One Octave |
| **Rhythm and Meter**<br>- Notes & Rests: dotted eighth, sixteenth<br><br><br>- Time Signatures: 2/4, 3/4 and 4/4<br>  - bar lines, notes and rests<br>- Upbeat (anacrusis) | **Rhythm and Meter Covered**<br>- Notes and Rests - including whole, half, dotted half, quarter, dotted quarter and eighth<br>* Workbook Pages - Eighth & Sixteenth Notes; Dotted Notes and Dotted Rests (Function of the Dot in Notes and Rests)<br>- Time Signatures: 2/4, 3/4 and 4/4; bar lines, notes and rests<br>* Workbook Pages - Adding Rests<br>* Workbook Pages - Time Signatures - Upbeat (Anacrusis); Adding Bar Lines; Rhythm Review |
| **Intervals**<br>- Melodic and Harmonic intervals up to and including an octave (using Key Signatures or Accidentals above the Tonic of the required keys)<br>- Perfect 1, 4, 5, 8; Major 2, 3, 6, 7; minor 3 | **Intervals Covered**<br>- Melodic and Harmonic Intervals (numerical size only)<br>* Workbook Pages - Identifying and Writing Intervals (Perfect 1, 4, 5, 8; Major 2, 3, 6, 7; minor 3) with and without a Key Signatures (using accidentals when needed); Melodic and Harmonic Intervals |
| **Scales and Scale Degree Names**<br>- Scales using Key Signatures and/or Accidentals:<br>Major: C, G, D, F, B-flat<br>Minor (natural, harmonic and melodic): a, e, b, d, g<br>- Scale Degree Names: Tonic, Subdominant, Dominant, Leading Tone and Subtonic | **Scales and Scale Degree Names Covered**<br>- Scales using Key Signatures and/or Accidentals:<br>Major: C, G, D, F, B-flat<br>Minor (natural, harmonic and melodic): a, e, b, d, g<br>* Workbook Pages - Major and Minor (Natural, Harmonic and Melodic) Scales and Scale Degrees<br>* Workbook Pages - Scale Degree Names: Lower Tonic, Mediant, Subdominant, Dominant, Leading Tone, Upper Tonic and Subtonic |
| **Chords**<br>- Tonic and Dominant Triads of required keys in Root Position (solid/blocked or broken form)<br><br><br>- Functional Chord Symbols (I, i, V)<br><br>- Root/Quality Chord Symbols (ex. C, Am) | **Chords Covered**<br>- Tonic Triads of required keys in Root Position (solid/blocked or broken form)<br>* Workbook Pages - Tonic and Dominant Triads in Major and harmonic minor scales (solid/blocked, broken ascending and broken descending)<br>* Workbook Pages - Functional Chord Symbols - Tonic and Dominant Triads in Major and Relative minor keys (Solid/blocked and broken)<br>* Workbook Pages - Root/Quality Chord Symbols - Tonic and Dominant Triads in Major and Relative minor keys |

**\* Supplemental Workbook Pages - New concepts introduced in the 2016 RCM Syllabus.**

## RCM Level 3 Theory Concept (Continued)

### Analysis
- Identification of concepts from this level and the previous levels within short music examples
- Melodic phrases: same (a), similar (a1) or different (b)

### Melody and Composition
- Composition of a short melody in a Major Key with a given rhythm
   - Use steps, skips and leaps (between notes of the Tonic and Dominant triads)
   - End on scale degree 1̂ or 3̂

### Musical Terms and Signs
- Tempo, Dynamics and Articulation

### Music History/Appreciation
- An Introduction to the family life of J.S. Bach
- The Anna Magdalena Notebook
- Baroque Dances (Menuet, Gavotte and Gigue)
- The Harpsichord

- Menuet in G Major, BWV Anh. 114 (by Christian Petzold)
Listening Focus: Character of the dance (tempo, meter, rhythmic features)
- French Suite No. 5 in G Major, BWV 817 (by J.S. Bach) - Gavotte and Gigue
Listening Focus: Character of each dance (tempo, meter, rhythmic features)

### Examination
(No Level 3 Theory Exam)

## Ultimate Music Theory Prep 2 Workbook (Continued)

### Analysis Covered
* Workbook Pages - Identification and writing of concepts from this level and the previous levels within short music examples
* Workbook Pages - Analysis of Melody - Melodic Phrases - same (a), similar (a1) or different (b)

### Melody and Composition Covered
* Workbook Page - Melody Writing - Leaps Between Notes of the Tonic and Dominant Triads
* Workbook Page - Melody Writing - Ending on Stable Scale Degrees 1̂ or 3̂
* Workbook Page - Analysis and Melody Writing - Motive Patterns (repetition, rhythmic and/or melodic) and Phrases
* Workbook Page Bonus - Imagine, Compose, Explore

### Musical Terms and Signs Covered
* Workbook Pages - Musical Terms and Signs
* Workbook Page Bonus - Analysis and Sight Reading

### Music History/Appreciation Covered
* Workbook Page - J.S. Bach
* Workbook Page - The Anna Magdalena Notebook
* Workbook Page - Baroque Dances
* Workbook Page - The Harpsichord

* Workbook Page - Menuet in G Major, BWV Anh. 114 (by Christian Petzold)
Listening Focus: Character of the dance (tempo, meter, rhythmic features); Baroque Ornamentation (Trill, Mordent, Appoggiatura)
* Workbook Pages - French Suite No. 5 in G Major, BWV 817 (by J.S. Bach) - Gavotte and Gigue
Listening Focus: Character of each dance (tempo, meter, rhythmic features); Polyphonic Texture

### Review Tests & Final Exam
- 12 Accumulative Review Tests (1 with each of the 12 Lessons)
*UMT LEVEL 3 THEORY EXAM

**UltimateMusicTheoryApp.com** - Over 7000 Flashcards including audio! 6 Subjects: Beginner - Prep, Basic, Intermediate, Advanced, Ear Training & Music Trivia (including History).

Beginner Music Theory App Subject - Use with the Prep 1 and Prep 2 Workbooks

12 Decks - 1,325 Cards - See, hear and identify notes on the staff, scales, triads and musical terms. Learn notation including note and rest values, Key Signatures, 4/4 Simple Time & more!

- 1 - Notation, Landmarks and Ledger Lines
- 2 - Note & Rest Values and Intervals
- 3 - Simple Time Signatures
- 4 - Semitones, Whole tones & Accidentals
- 5 - Major scales - 2 sharps & 2 flats
- 6 - Natural minor scales - 2 sharps & 2 flats
- 7 - Key Signatures - 2 sharps & 2 flats
- 8 - Key Signatures on the Grand Staff
- 9 - Major Triads - solid and broken
- 10 - Harmonic minor scales
- 11 - Melodic minor scales
- 12 - Analysis and Musical Terms

## NOTES - EIGHTH and SIXTEENTH

Each **note** has a specific time value of **sound**. Each **rest** has a specific time value of **silence**.

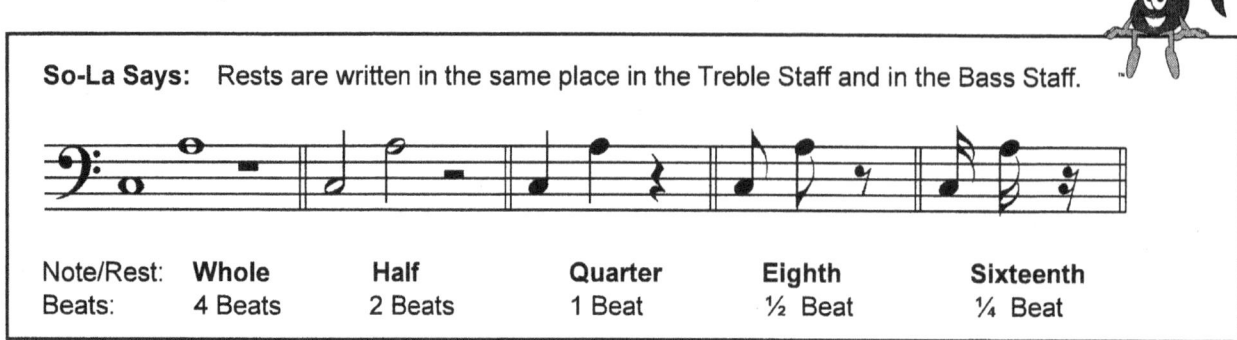

| Note/Rest: | **Whole** | **Half** | **Quarter** | **Eighth** | **Sixteenth** |
|---|---|---|---|---|---|
| Beats: | 4 Beats | 2 Beats | 1 Beat | ½ Beat | ¼ Beat |

1. a) Following the example above, write the notes and rests in the Bass Clef.
   b) Write the number of beats each note/rest receives.

| Note/Rest: | **Whole** | **Half** | **Quarter** | **Eighth** | **Sixteenth** |
|---|---|---|---|---|---|
| Beats: | 4 Beats | 2 Beats | 1 Beat | 1/2 Beat | 1/4 Beat |

Eighth notes and sixteenth notes can be **beamed together** in combinations that equal one beat (one Basic Beat of a quarter note).

A **SINGLE BEAM** is used when two or more ♫ eighth notes are joined together.

A **DOUBLE BEAM** is used when two or more ♬ sixteenth notes are joined together.

Different combinations of note values may be beamed together.

♪ **Ti-Do Tip:** The notehead furthest away from the third line (the middle line) determines the direction of all the stems.

2. Copy the following:

## RHYTHM REVIEW - BEAMS

Eighth notes and sixteenth notes can be **beamed together** in groups that equal one Quarter Note.
One Quarter Note = One Basic Beat.

♪ **Ti-Do Tip:** One (single) flag = an eighth note; two (double) flags = sixteenth note.
One (single) beam = eighth notes; two (double) beams = sixteenth notes.

1. Rewrite the notes using the correct beams.

**So-La Says:** Use **Scoops** to help join beams together into each Quarter Note Basic Beat.

Not Beamed: = Beamed:

Scoop:

2. a) In line 1, scoop each quarter note Basic Beat.
   b) Rewrite each rhythm in the measure below in line 2, beaming the notes into Basic Beats.
   c) In line 2, scoop each quarter note Basic Beat.

Scoop:

Scoop:

# FUNCTION OF A DOT in NOTES

Dotted Note: A **dot** placed after a note adds **"half the value"** of the note.

> When a quarter note equals one Basic Beat, the number of beats for the dotted notes are:
>
> ♪. = ♪ + ♬ = ¾ of a beat     ♩. = ♩ + ♪ = 1½ beats     ♩. = ♩ + ♩ = 3 beats
> Dotted Eighth Note           Dotted Quarter Note        Dotted Half Note

1. a) Below the dotted note in each measure, write the note and the note value of the dot.
   b) Write the number of beats for each dotted note.

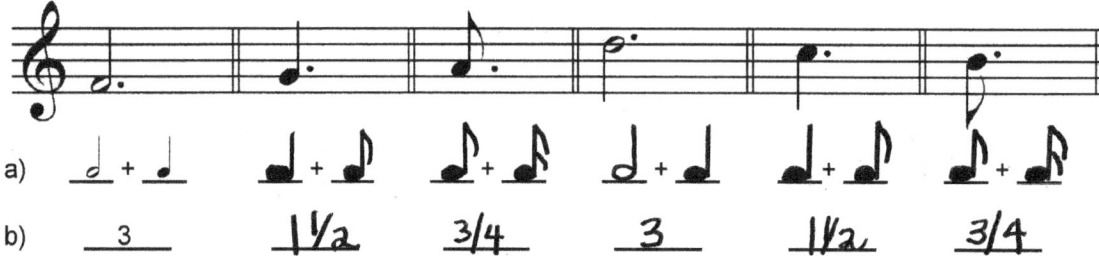

a) ♩ + ♩    ♩ + ♪    ♪ + ♬    ♩ + ♩    ♩ + ♪    ♪ + ♬

b)   3     1½     3/4     3     1½     3/4

> **So-La Says:** The dot is written behind (after) the note in the same space for a space note, and in the space above for a line note.
>
>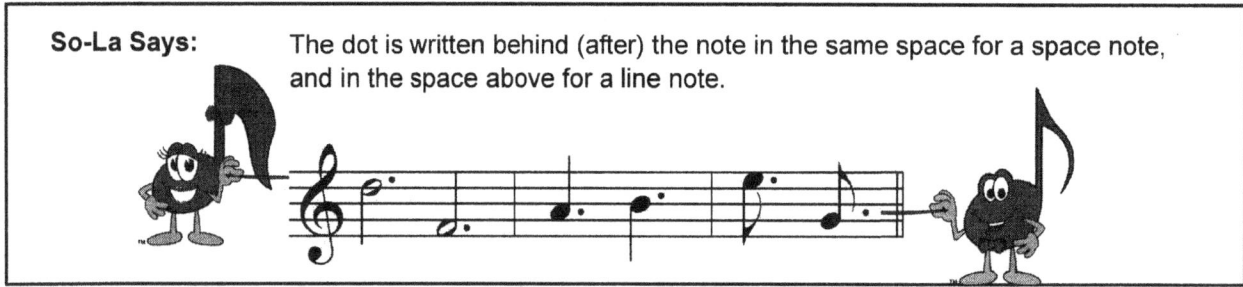

♪ **Ti-Do Tip:** A Stem is approximately one octave in length. Stem Rules for when the notehead is:

**ABOVE** the middle line, stem DOWN on the left: 'ρ' like 'p' in → *pizza*
**ON** the middle line, stem DOWN on the left or UP on the right:
**BELOW** the middle line, stem UP on the right: 'd' like 'd' in → *donuts*

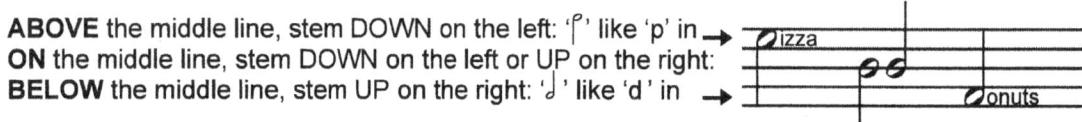

2. Add a stem and a dot to each notehead to create a dotted quarter note.

3. Copy the following:

# FUNCTION OF A DOT in RESTS

Dotted Rest: A **dot** placed after a rest adds **"half the value"** of the rest.

> When a quarter note equals one Basic Beat, the number of beats for the dotted rests are:
>
> 𝄾· = 𝄾 + 𝄿 = ¾ of a beat     𝄽· = 𝄽 + 𝄾 = 1½ beats     ▬· = ▬ + 𝄽 = 3 beats
>
> Dotted Eighth Rest            Dotted Quarter Rest            Dotted Half Rest

1. Write the matching note for each rest. Write how many beats each rest/note receives.

   a) ▬·  and  𝅗𝅥·          b) 𝄾·  and  ♪·          c) 𝄽·  and  𝅘𝅥·
   
   = __3__ beats each       = __3/4__ of a beat each       = __1½__ beats each

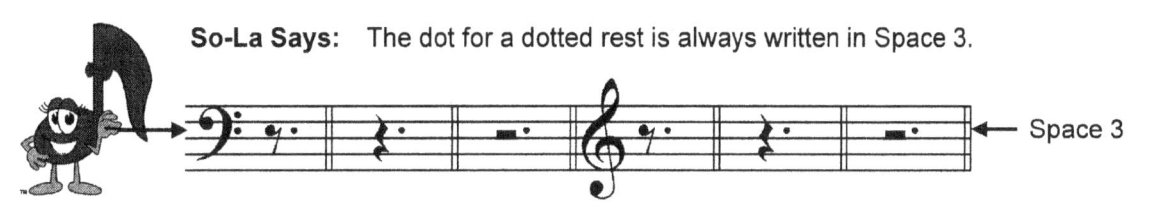

**So-La Says:** The dot for a dotted rest is always written in Space 3.

← Space 3

♫ **Ti-Do Tip:** Party Space 3 is the place to be, when you are a dot for a rest!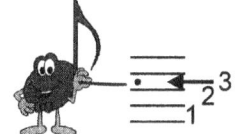

2. Write the following rests in the Treble Staff and in the Bass Staff.

   a) Dotted Half Rest        b) Dotted Quarter Rest        c) Dotted Eighth Rest

3. a) Add a dot to each note to create a dotted note and to each rest to create a dotted rest.
   b) Write the number of beats for each dotted note and for each dotted rest.

Beats:  __3__    __1½__    __3/4__    __3__    __1½__    __3/4__

# RHYTHM REVIEW - ADDING RESTS

**Eighth notes**, **dotted eighth notes** and **sixteenth notes** can also be combined with **rests** to equal one beat (one Basic Beat of a quarter note).

1. Write the total number of beats in each measure.

Beats: 1   1   1   1   1   1   1   1

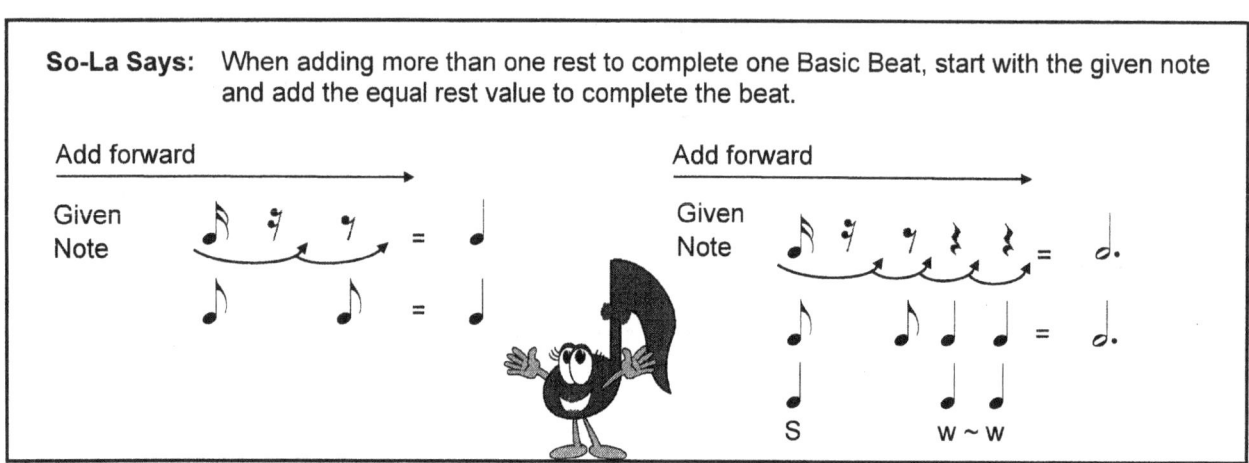

**So-La Says:** When adding more than one rest to complete one Basic Beat, start with the given note and add the equal rest value to complete the beat.

♫ **Ti-Do Tip:** When adding rests to complete a measure, **complete one Basic Beat at a time**.

2. Indicate whether the rests in each measure are Correct or Incorrect.

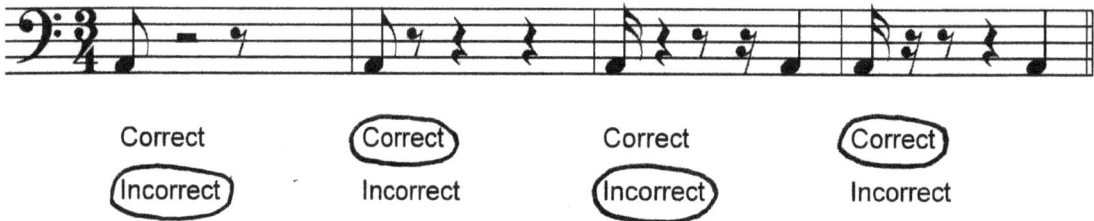

   Correct            (Correct)         Correct           (Correct)
   (Incorrect)         Incorrect        (Incorrect)         Incorrect

3. a) Scoop each Quarter Note Basic Beat.
   b) Write the Basic Beat and the pulse below each measure.
   c) Add one rest below each bracket to complete each measure.

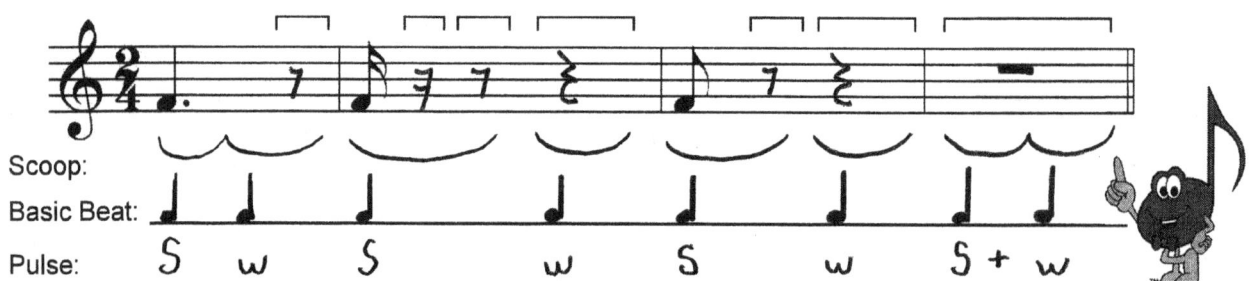

Scoop:
Basic Beat:  ♩  ♩   ♩  ♩   ♩  ♩   ♩  ♩
Pulse:       S  w   S  w   S  w   S + w

# RHYTHM REVIEW - ADDING RESTS

When adding rests to complete a measure, **complete one Basic Beat at a time**.

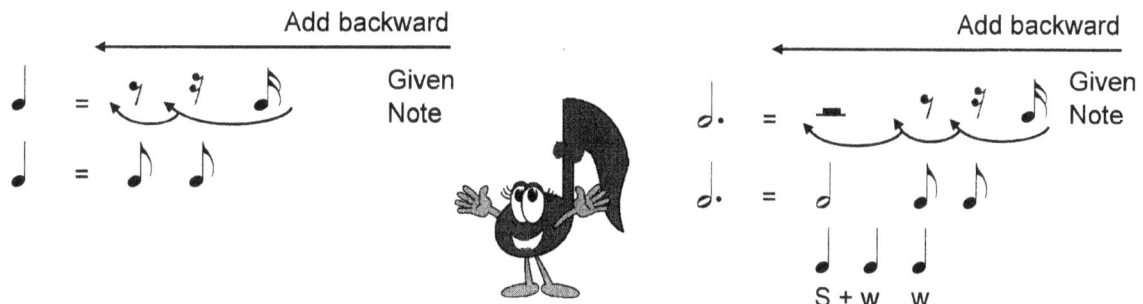

**So-La Says:** When adding more than one rest to complete one Basic Beat, start with the given note and add the equal rest value to complete the beat.

Although we now understand the value and purpose of the dot, we do not use dotted rests when completing measures in Simple Time with rests.

♫ **Ti-Do Tip:** Use a Whole Rest for a whole measure of silence in $\frac{2}{4}$, $\frac{3}{4}$ and $\frac{4}{4}$ time.

1. a) Scoop each Quarter Note Basic Beat.
   b) Write the Basic Beat and the pulse below each measure.
   c) Add one rest below each bracket to complete each measure.

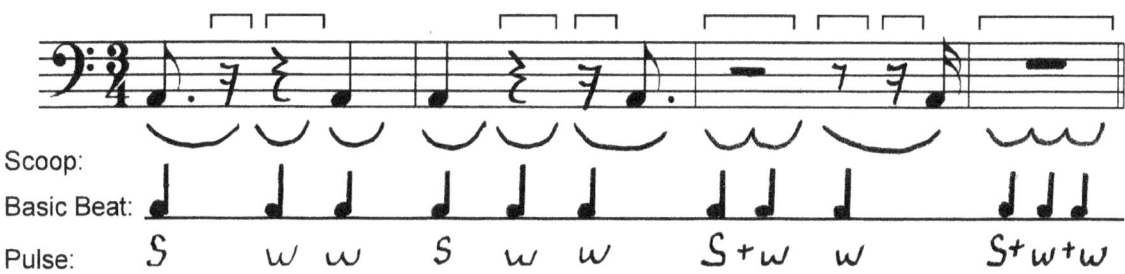

# TIME SIGNATURES - UPBEAT (ANACRUSIS)

An **Anacrusis**, **Pickup** or **Upbeat** is a note or group of notes (or rests) in the first incomplete measure at the beginning of the music. The last (final) measure at the end of the music will also be an incomplete measure. Together they equal one complete measure. The downbeat is the first strong beat in a measure.

**Measure numbers** are written in boxes above the first count in the measure: 1.

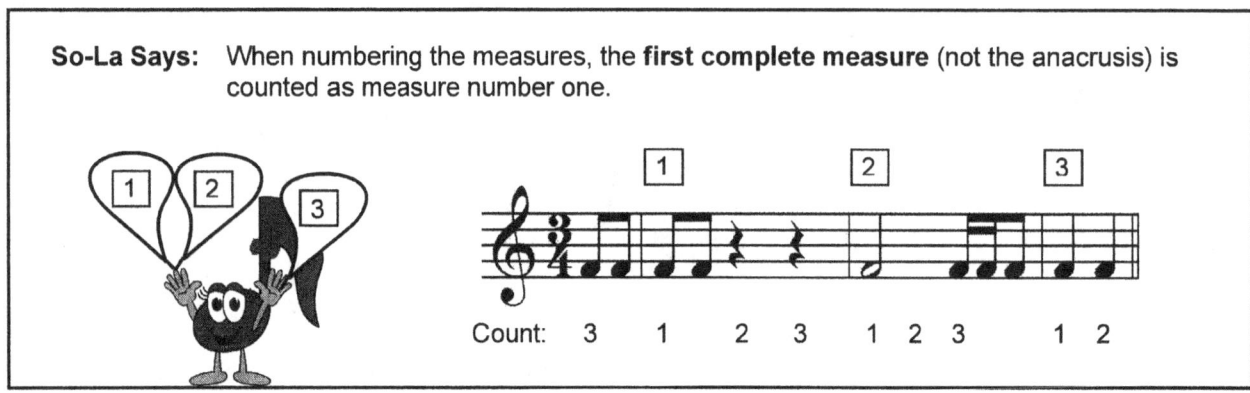

1. a) Add the correct Time Signature below each bracket.
   b) Write the counts below each measure.
   c) Write the measure numbers in the square box at the beginning of each measure.

♫ **Ti-Do Time:** COUNT out loud and CLAP each rhythm.

To "clap" a rest, open your hands (and do not clap them together) for the value of the rest.

# RHYTHM REVIEW - ADDING BAR LINES

When **adding Bar Lines**, look at the Time Signature. Look for the first complete measure. Watch out for an Anacrusis (incomplete measure). Not all rhythms will begin with a full (complete) measure.

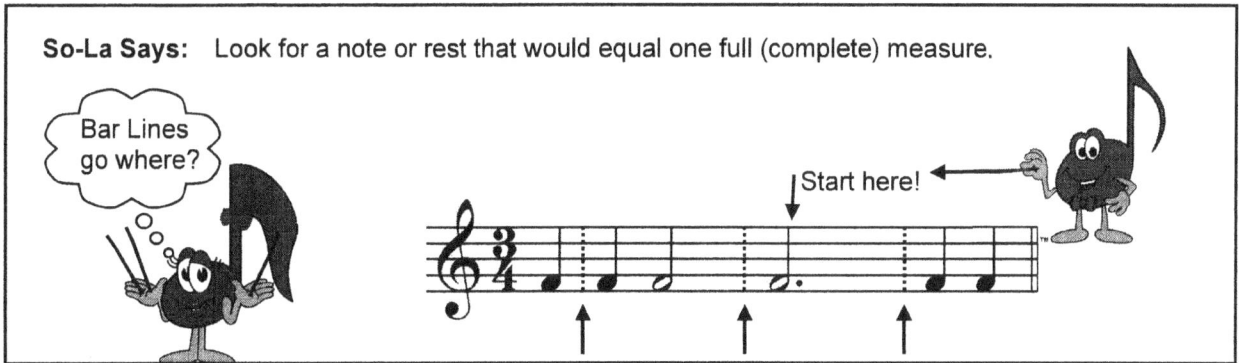

♫ **Ti-Do Tip:** A **Bar Line** is written from the top (line 5) to the bottom (line 1) of the staff.

1. a) Scoop each Basic Beat.
   b) Add bar lines.
   c) Write the Basic Beat below the Scoop.
   d) Write the counts below each Basic Beat.

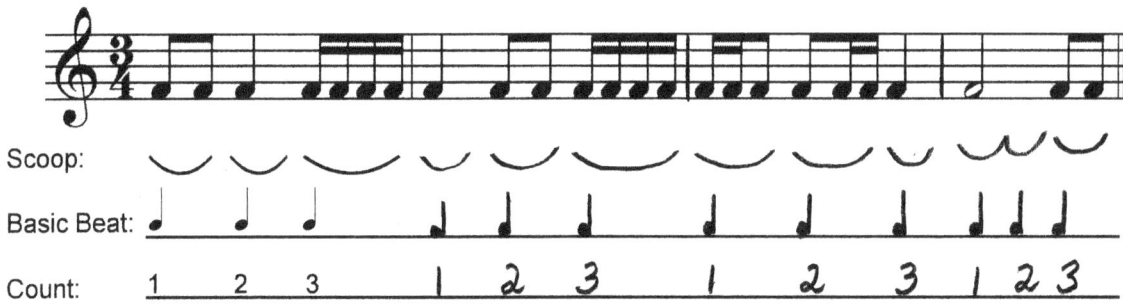

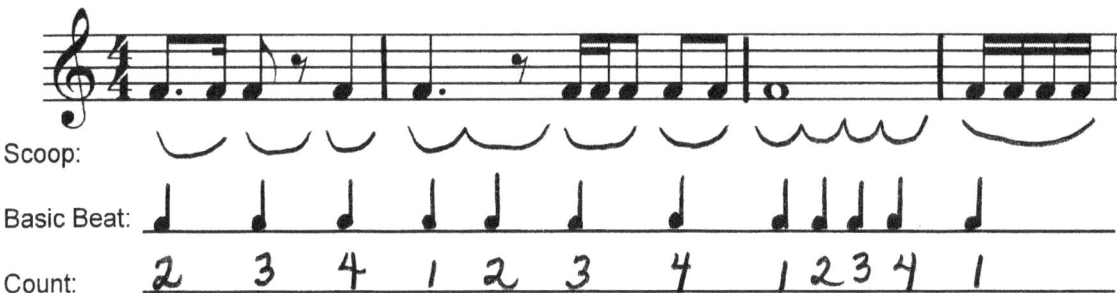

♫ **Ti-Do Time:** TAP the Basic Beat with your foot while you CLAP each rhythm.

COUNT out loud while you TAP and CLAP.

## MAJOR SCALES and SCALE DEGREES

A **Major scale** is a series of 8 notes in a specific pattern:

$\hat{1}$ whole step $\hat{2}$ whole step $\hat{3}$ half step $\hat{4}$ whole step $\hat{5}$ whole step $\hat{6}$ whole step $\hat{7}$ half step $\hat{8}$ ($\hat{1}$).

**Scale Degree Numbers** are numbers with a circumflex, caret sign or hat ( ˆ ) written above the number. Scale Degree Numbers are written below the notes of a scale.

**So-La Says:** **Scale Degree Names** are names given to the specific scale degree numbers.

The **Tonic** $\hat{1}$ is the first note of the scale (establishing the tonality).

The **Subdominant** $\hat{4}$ is a 5th below the Upper Tonic (sub = below).

The **Dominant** $\hat{5}$ is a 5th above the Lower Tonic.

The **Leading Tone** $\hat{7}$ is a 2nd (half step) below the Upper Tonic (leading up to the Tonic).

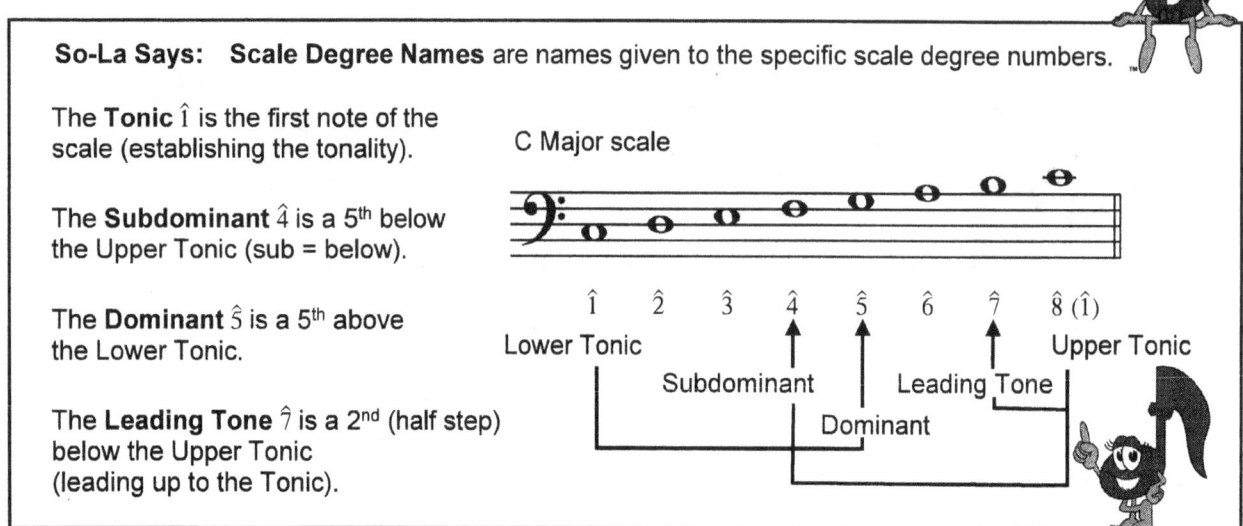

♫ **Ti-Do Tip:** A Whole Step is also called a Whole Tone; a Half Step is also called a Semitone.

1. Write the Scale Degree Numbers below the notes of the G Major scale.

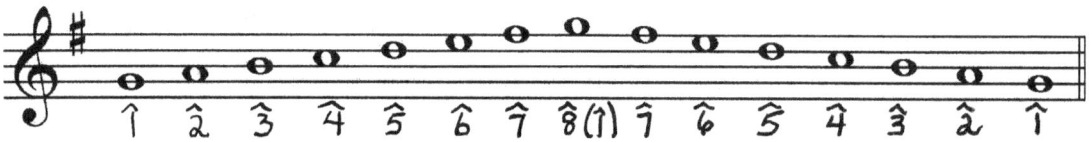

2. Below each scale, label each Tonic (T), Subdominant (SD), Dominant (D) and Leading Tone (LT).

   a) B flat Major scale

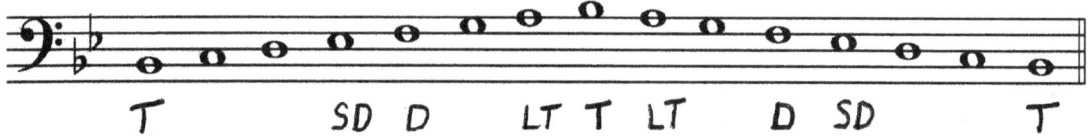

   b) D Major scale

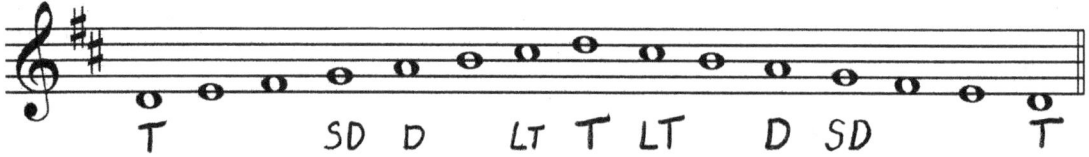

# MINOR SCALES - NATURAL MINOR and SCALE DEGREES

A **Natural minor scale** is a series of 8 notes in a specific pattern:

$\hat{1}$ whole step $\hat{2}$ half step $\hat{3}$ whole step $\hat{4}$ whole step $\hat{5}$ half step $\hat{6}$ whole step $\hat{7}$ whole step $\hat{8}$ ($\hat{1}$).

In the Natural Form of a minor scale, nothing is changed (added).

The 7th note of the natural minor scale is called the **Subtonic**. It is a whole step (whole tone) below the Tonic (Upper Tonic).

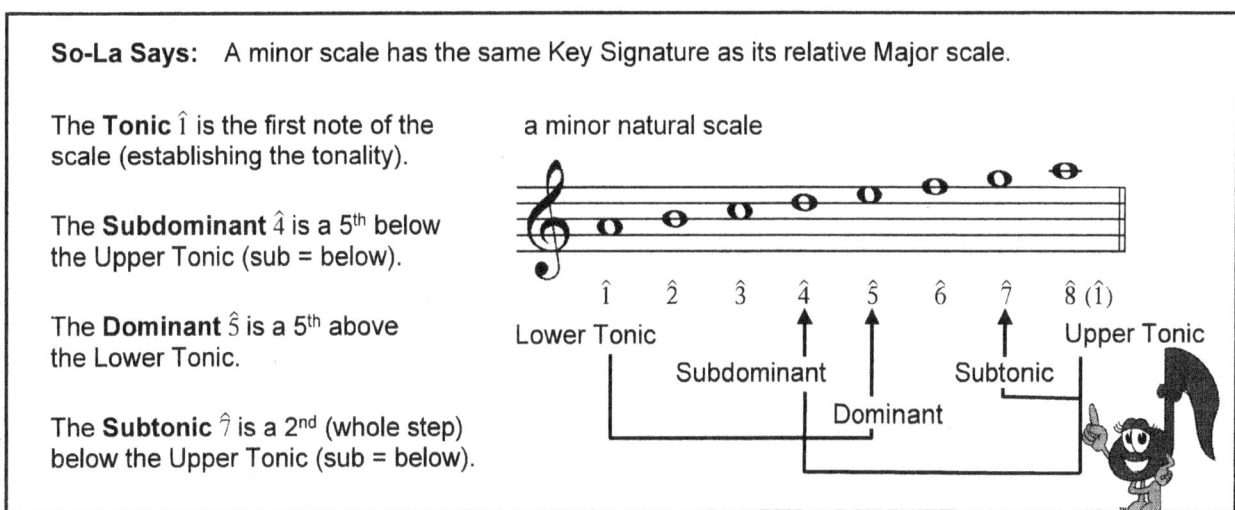

**So-La Says:** A minor scale has the same Key Signature as its relative Major scale.

The **Tonic** $\hat{1}$ is the first note of the scale (establishing the tonality).

The **Subdominant** $\hat{4}$ is a 5th below the Upper Tonic (sub = below).

The **Dominant** $\hat{5}$ is a 5th above the Lower Tonic.

The **Subtonic** $\hat{7}$ is a 2nd (whole step) below the Upper Tonic (sub = below).

♪ **Ti-Do Tip:** A Leading Tone is a half step below the Tonic. A Subtonic is a whole step below the Tonic.

1. Below each scale, label each Tonic (T), Subdominant (SD), Dominant (D) and Subtonic (SBT).

   a) g minor natural scale

   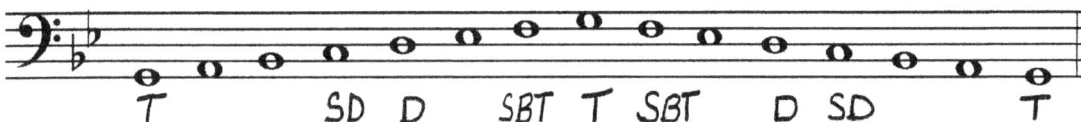

   b) b minor natural scale

   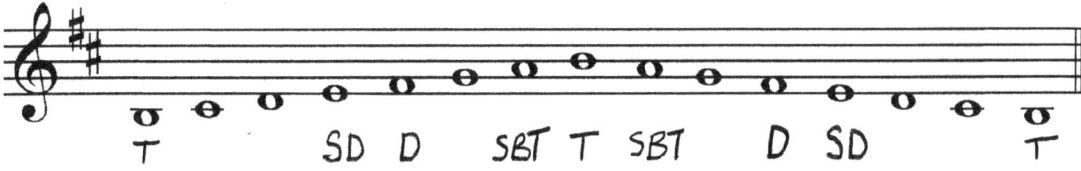

♪ **Ti-Do Time:** LISTEN as your Teacher plays the scales in the Exercises on Pages 16 and 17.

Identify if the scale played is a Major scale or a natural minor scale.

# MINOR SCALES - HARMONIC MINOR and SCALE DEGREES

A **Harmonic minor scale** is a series of 8 notes in a specific pattern:

$\hat{1}$ whole step $\hat{2}$ half step $\hat{3}$ whole step $\hat{4}$ whole step $\hat{5}$ half step $\hat{6}$ whole + half step $\hat{7}$ half step $\hat{8}$ ($\hat{1}$).

In the Harmonic Form of a minor scale, the 7th note is raised one chromatic half step ascending (going up) and descending (going down).

The 7th note of the harmonic minor scale is called the **Leading Tone**. It is a half step (semitone) below the Tonic (Upper Tonic).

> **So-La Says:** The raised 7th of the harmonic minor scale is written as an accidental in the scale.
>
> Accidentals apply to all notes on the same line or in the same space until canceled by a bar line or by another accidental.

The **Tonic** $\hat{1}$ is the first note of the scale (establishing the tonality).

The **Subdominant** $\hat{4}$ is a 5th below the Upper Tonic (sub = below).

The **Dominant** $\hat{5}$ is a 5th above the Lower Tonic.

The **Leading Tone** $\hat{7}$ is a 2nd (half step) below the Upper Tonic (leading up to the Tonic).

♫ **Ti-Do Tip:** A Leading Tone is a half step below the Tonic. A Subtonic is a whole step below the Tonic.

1. Below each scale, label each Tonic (T), Subdominant (SD), Dominant (D) and Leading Tone (LT).

   a) g minor harmonic scale

   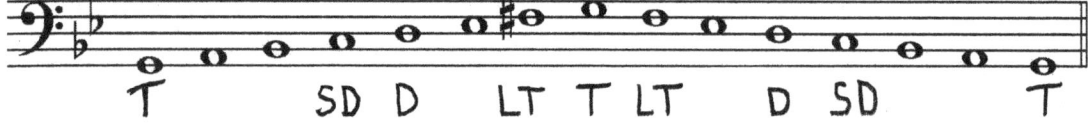

   b) b minor harmonic scale

   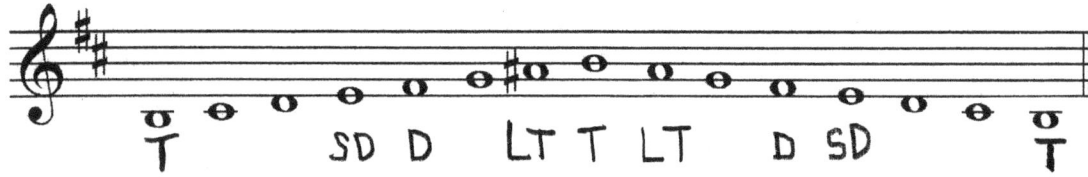

# MINOR SCALES - MELODIC MINOR and SCALE DEGREES

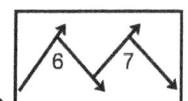

A **Melodic minor scale** is a series of 8 notes in a specific ascending and descending pattern.

In the ascending melodic minor scale, the 6th and 7th notes are raised. The pattern is:

$\hat{1}$ whole step $\hat{2}$ half step $\hat{3}$ whole step $\hat{4}$ whole step $\hat{5}$ whole step $\hat{6}$ whole step $\hat{7}$ half step $\hat{8}$ ($\hat{1}$).

In the descending melodic minor scale, the 6th and 7th notes are lowered. The pattern is:

$\hat{8}$ ($\hat{1}$) whole step $\hat{7}$ whole step $\hat{6}$ half step $\hat{5}$ whole step $\hat{4}$ whole step $\hat{3}$ half step $\hat{2}$ whole step $\hat{1}$.

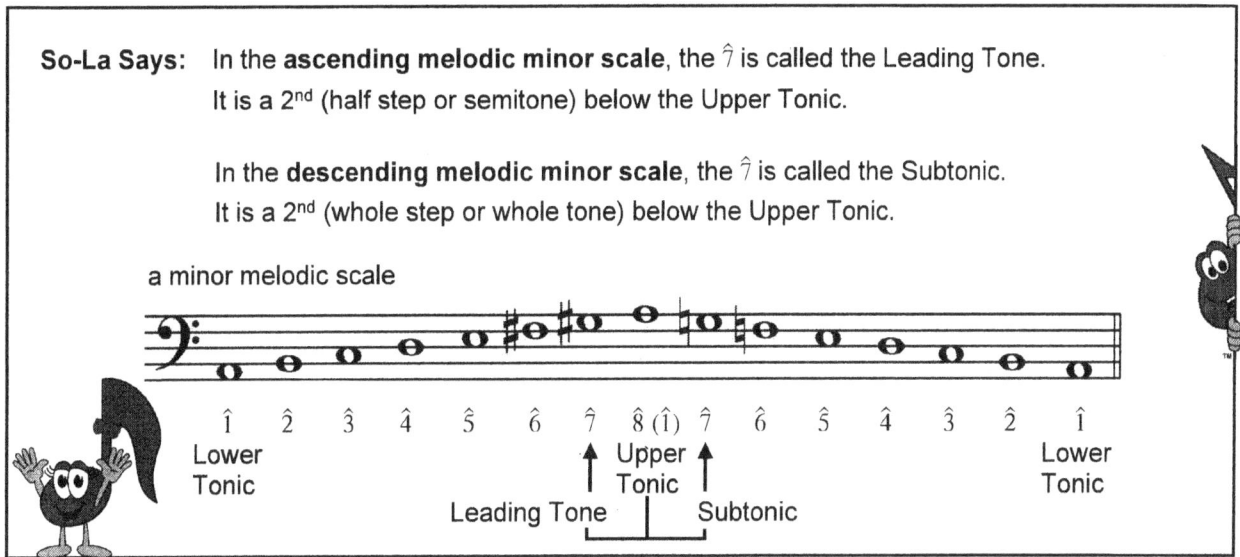

**So-La Says:** In the **ascending melodic minor scale**, the $\hat{7}$ is called the Leading Tone.
It is a 2nd (half step or semitone) below the Upper Tonic.

In the **descending melodic minor scale**, the $\hat{7}$ is called the Subtonic.
It is a 2nd (whole step or whole tone) below the Upper Tonic.

a minor melodic scale

♫ **Ti-Do Tip:** The descending melodic minor scale is the same as the natural minor scale.

1. Below each scale, label each Tonic (T), Subdominant (SD), Dominant (D), Leading Tone (LT) and Subtonic (SBT).

    a) g minor melodic scale

    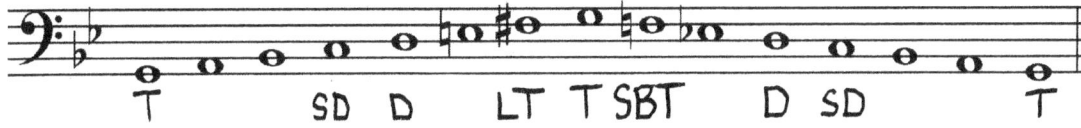

    b) b minor melodic scale

    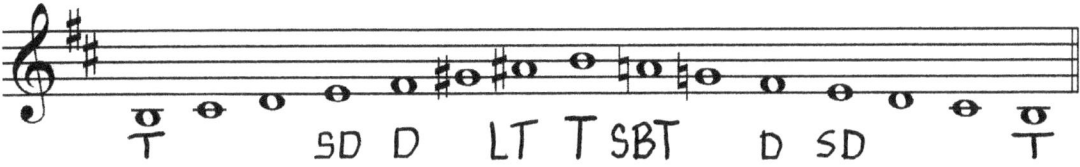

# INTERVALS - PERFECT and MAJOR

An **Interval** is the distance in pitch between two notes. Numbers (1, 2, 3, etc.) are used to identify the size of the interval. To identify the interval, count each line and each space from the lowest note to the highest note. The lowest note is always counted as 1.

Perfect Intervals are 1, 4, 5 and 8. The abbreviation for Perfect is "Per".

Major Intervals are 2, 3, 6 and 7. The abbreviation for Major is "Maj".

Intervals are based on the notes of the Major scale. When naming intervals, the lower note of the interval is the Tonic of the Major key.

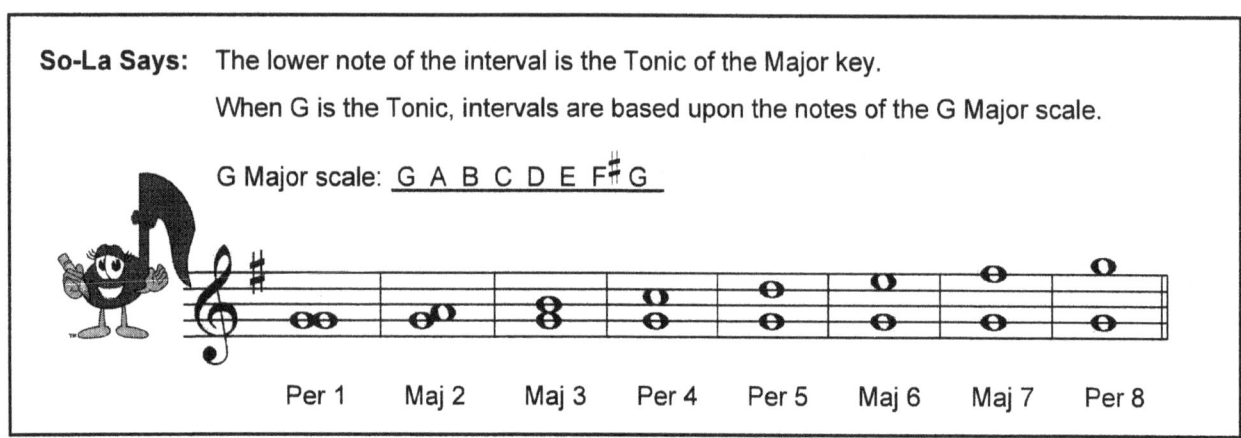

♪ **Ti-Do Tip:** The **size** of the interval is the interval number.
The **quality** of the interval is whether it is Major or Perfect.

1. a) Write the notes of the Major scale above the staff.
   b) Identify the size (number) and quality (Maj or Per) of each interval below the staff.

B♭ Major scale:  B♭ C D E♭ F G A B♭

Per 1   Maj 2   Maj 3   Per 4   Per 5   Maj 6   Maj 7   Per 8

D Major scale: D E F# G A B C# D

Per 1   Maj 2   Maj 3   Per 4   Per 5   Maj 6   Maj 7   Per 8

## INTERVALS - MAJOR and MINOR THIRDS

Intervals found in the Major scale (Per 1, Maj 2, Maj 3, Per 4, Per 5, Maj 6, Maj 7 and Per 8) are called **Diatonic Intervals**. Intervals may be harmonic or melodic.

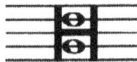

**HARMONIC** Interval - H is for Harmony
Two notes - one ABOVE the other (together)

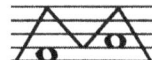

**MELODIC** Interval - M is for Melody
Two notes - one BESIDE the other (separate)

A **Major third** (Maj 3) is the interval from the Tonic to the 3rd (the Mediant or $\hat{3}$ scale degree) of the Major scale. A Major 3 is always 4 half steps (semitones).

When a Major third becomes one half step smaller (by lowering the upper note of the interval one half step), it is called a **minor third**. A minor 3 is always 3 half steps (semitones).

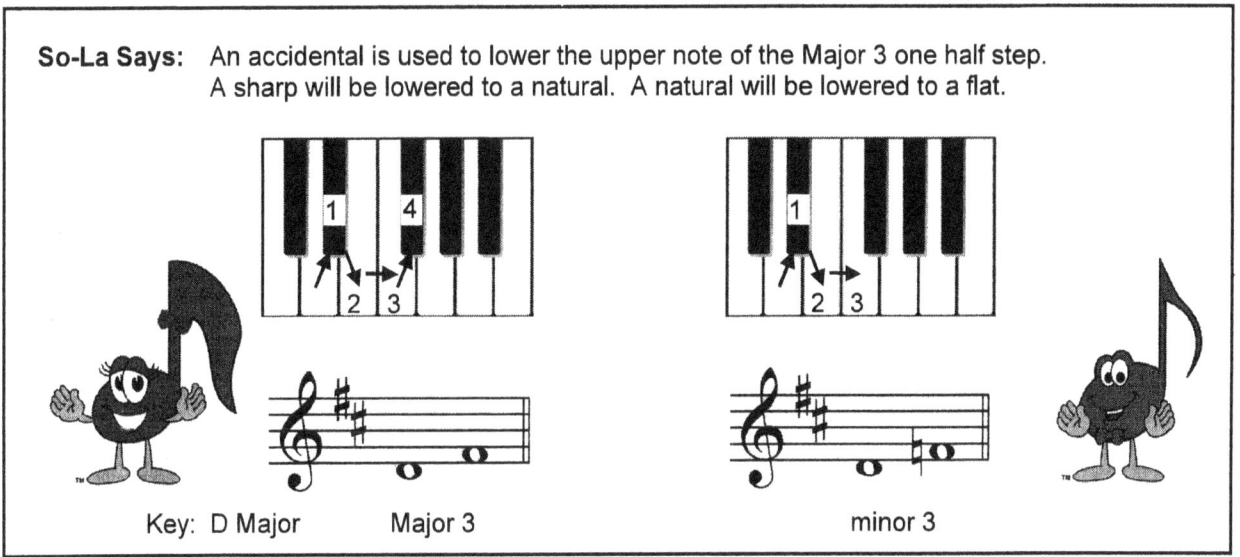

**So-La Says:** An accidental is used to lower the upper note of the Major 3 one half step. A sharp will be lowered to a natural. A natural will be lowered to a flat.

Key: D Major     Major 3          minor 3

♫ **Ti-Do Tip:** A Key Signature is canceled by writing another Key Signature. It is not necessary to cancel a Key Signature using naturals. Simply write the sharps or flats of the new Key.

1. a) Name the Major key for each measure.
   b) Rewrite each Major third as a minor third by using an accidental to lower the upper note one half step. Use whole notes.

Major 3   minor 3     Major 3   minor 3     Major 3   minor 3

Major key: __D Major__     Major key: __B♭ Major__     Major key: __G Major__

# WRITING MAJOR and PERFECT INTERVALS - USING KEY SIGNATURES (Root is Tonic)

An interval is always based on the notes of the Major scale (Major Key Signature) of the lower (Root) note of the interval.

When the lower (Root) note of the interval is the Tonic note of the Key Signature, accidentals will not be needed to write a Major (2, 3, 6, 7) Interval or a Perfect (1, 4, 5, 8) Interval.

> **So-La's Steps to Writing a Major or Perfect Interval Using a Key Signature (Root is Tonic)**
>
> Follow So-La's Steps to write a Major 6 above the given note.
>
> **Step 1:** Identify the Major Key Signature. Name the given (Root) note.
>
> Key Signature is B♭ Major (B♭ and E♭). Given (Root) note is B♭.
> B♭ is the Tonic note of the Major Key Signature.
>
> **Step 2:** Write the interval above the given note. Name the upper note.
>
> The interval is a 6th. Observing the Key Signature, the upper note is G.
> No further accidentals are needed. A Major 6th above B♭ is G.

♫ **Ti-Do Tip:** A Key Signature affects all the notes until the end of the line, or until changed by another Key Signature. Bar lines do not cancel a Key Signature.

1. a) Name the Major key. Name the Root note (the given note) of the Interval.
   b) Following "So-La's Steps to Writing a Major or Perfect Interval using a Key Signature", write the following melodic intervals. Use whole notes. Name the upper note of the Interval.

# WRITING a MINOR THIRD - USING KEY SIGNATURES (Root is Tonic)

An interval is always based on the notes of the Major scale (Major Key Signature) of the lower (Root) note of the interval.

To write an interval of a minor 3, when the lower (Root) note of the interval is the Tonic note of the Key Signature, an accidental will be needed to lower the third (the Mediant) one half step (semitone).

### So-La's Steps to Writing a minor Interval Using a Key Signature (Root is Tonic)

Follow the steps to write a minor 3 above the given note.

**Step 1:** Identify the Major Key Signature. Name the given (Root) note.

Key Signature is B♭ Major (B♭ and E♭). Given (Root) note is B♭.
B♭ is the Tonic note of the Major Key Signature.

**Step 2:** Write the Major 3rd above the given note. Name the upper note.

Observing the Key Signature, the upper note is D. In B♭ Major, the Key Signature is B♭ and E♭. A Major 3rd above B♭ is D.

**Step 3:** Lower the upper note one half step. This will need an accidental.

A minor 3rd above B♭ is D♭.

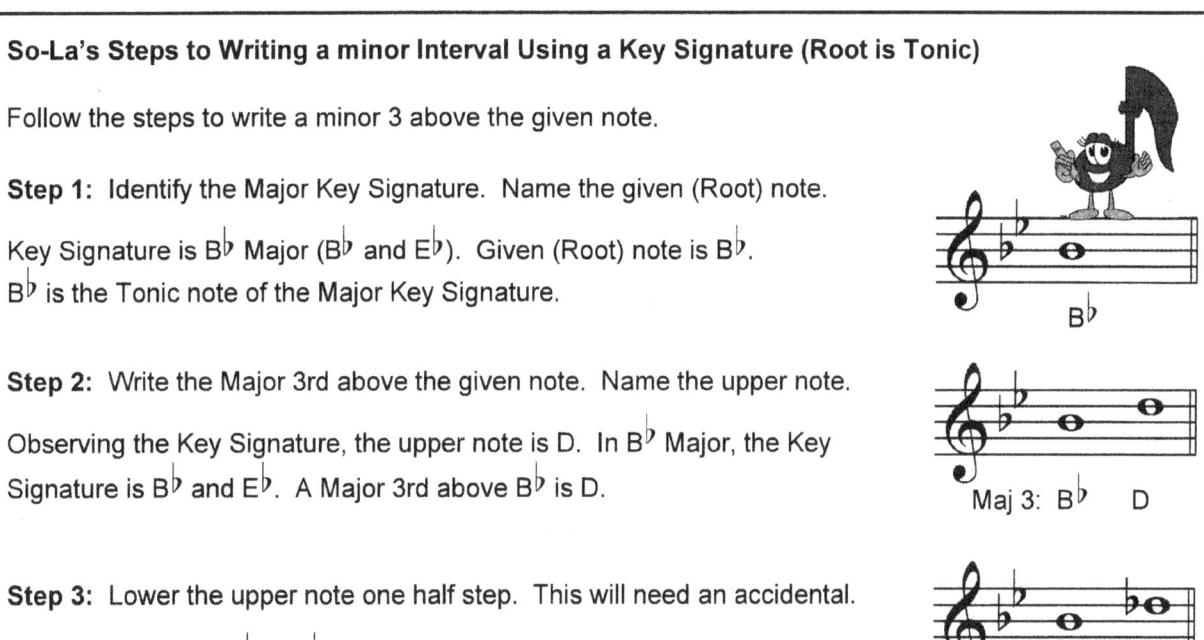

1. a) Name the Major key. Name the Root note (the given note) of the Interval.
   b) Following "So-La's Steps to Writing a minor Interval using a Key Signature", write the following melodic intervals. Use whole notes. Name the upper note of the Interval. Complete the Interval by adding an accidental when necessary.

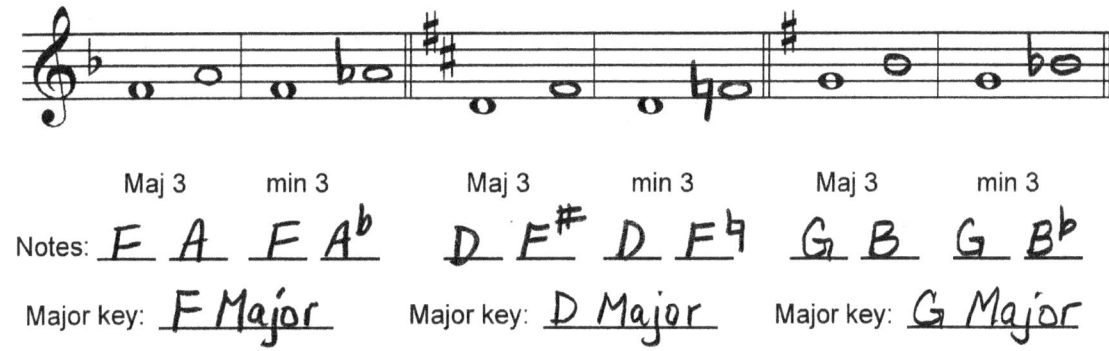

| | Maj 3 | min 3 | Maj 3 | min 3 | Maj 3 | min 3 |
|---|---|---|---|---|---|---|
| Notes: | F A | F A♭ | D F♯ | D F♮ | G B | G B♭ |
| Major key: | F Major | | D Major | | G Major | |

♪ **Ti-Do Time:** LISTEN as your Teacher plays the intervals in the Exercises on Pages 22 and 23.

Identify the name (size and quality) of each interval.

# WRITING MAJOR and PERFECT INTERVALS - USING KEY SIGNATURES (Root is NOT Tonic)

An interval is always based on the notes of the Major scale (Major Key Signature) of the lower (Root) note of the interval.

When the lower note of the interval is **NOT** the Tonic note of the Major Key Signature, accidentals may be needed to write a Major (2, 3, 6, 7) Interval or a Perfect (1, 4, 5, 8) Interval.

---

**So-La's Steps to Writing a Major or Perfect Interval Using a Key Signature (Root is NOT Tonic)**

Follow So-La's Steps to write a Major 6 above the given note.

**Step 1:** Identify the Major Key Signature. Name the given (Root) note.

Key Signature is B♭ Major (B♭ and E♭). Given (Root) note is D.
D is not the Tonic. (B♭ is the Tonic note of the Major Key Signature.)

**Step 2:** Write the interval above the given note. Name the upper note.

The Root note is D. The Key Signature for D Major is F♯ and C♯.
The note a 6th above D is B. According to the given Key Signature of B♭ Major, the note written a 6th above D is B♭. B is not flat in D Major.

**Step 3:** Complete the interval by adding an accidental when necessary.

In the key of D Major, a Major 6th above D is B. The given Key Signature indicates B♭. An accidental is necessary to change the B♭ to B♮.

---

♫ **Ti-Do Tip:** Observe the sharps or flats in the given Key Signature when identifying the Root note (the given note) and the note name for the Interval above the Root.

1. a) Name the Major key. Name the Root note (the given note) of the Interval.
   b) Following "So-La's Steps to Writing a Major or Perfect Interval using a Key Signature", write the following melodic intervals. Use whole notes. Name the upper note of the Interval. Complete the interval by adding an accidental when necessary.

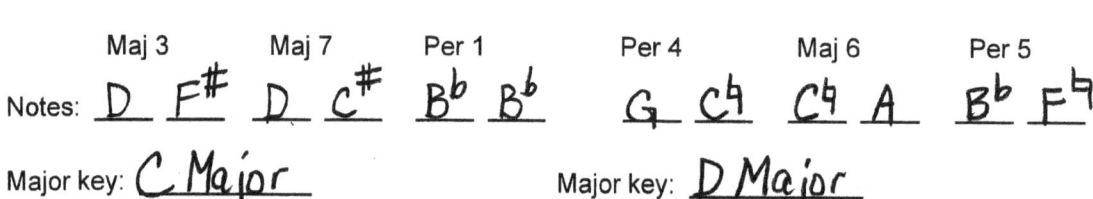

# WRITING a MINOR THIRD - USING KEY SIGNATURES (Root is NOT Tonic)

An interval is always based on the notes of the Major scale (Major Key Signature) of the lower (Root) note of the interval.

To write an interval of a minor 3, when the lower (Root) note of the interval is **NOT** the Tonic note of the Major Key Signature, an accidental may be needed to lower the third (the Mediant) one half step.

---

**So-La's Steps to Writing a minor Interval Using a Key Signature (Root is NOT Tonic)**

Follow the steps to write a minor 3 above the given note.

**Step 1:** Identify the Major Key Signature. Name the given note.

Key Signature is B♭ Major (B♭ and E♭). Given (Root) note is G.
G is not the Tonic. (B♭ is the Tonic note of the Major Key Signature.)

**Step 2:** Write the Major 3rd above the given note. Name the upper note.

Observing the Key Signature, the upper note is B♭. In G Major, the Key Signature is F♯. The Major 3rd above G is B♮.

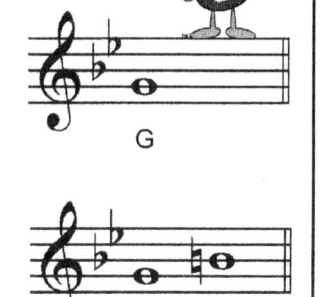

Maj 3: G   B♮

**Step 3:** Lower the upper note one half step. This may need an accidental.

A minor 3rd above G is B♭. The Key Signature contains a B♭, therefore no accidental is needed to write the minor 3rd.

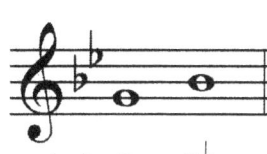

min 3: G   B♭

---

1. a) Name the Major key. Name the Root note (the given note) of the Interval.
   b) Following "So-La's Steps to Writing a minor Interval using a Key Signature", write the following melodic intervals. Use whole notes. Name the upper note of the Interval. Complete the Interval by adding an accidental when necessary.

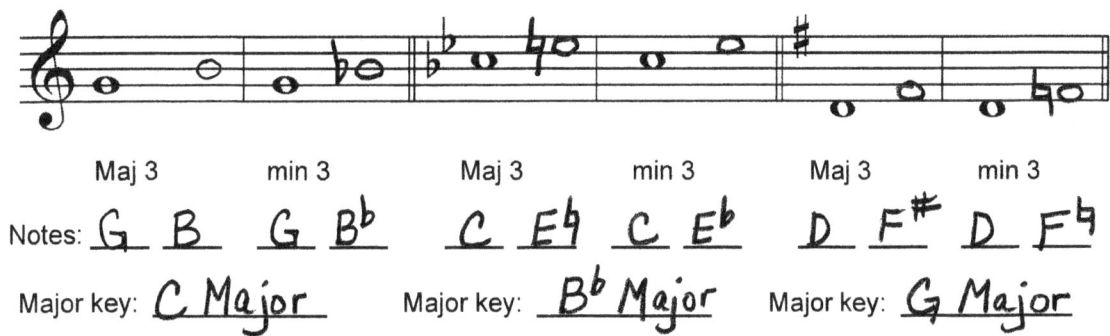

| Maj 3 | min 3 | Maj 3 | min 3 | Maj 3 | min 3 |

Notes: G  B     G  B♭     C  E♮     C  E♭     D  F♯     D  F♮

Major key: C Major          Major key: B♭ Major          Major key: G Major

---

🎵 **Ti-Do Time:** LISTEN as your Teacher plays the intervals in the Exercises on Pages 24 and 25.

Identify the name (size and quality) of each interval.

# WRITING INTERVALS - USING ACCIDENTALS

An interval is always based on the notes of the Major scale (Major Key Signature) of the lower (Root) note of the interval.

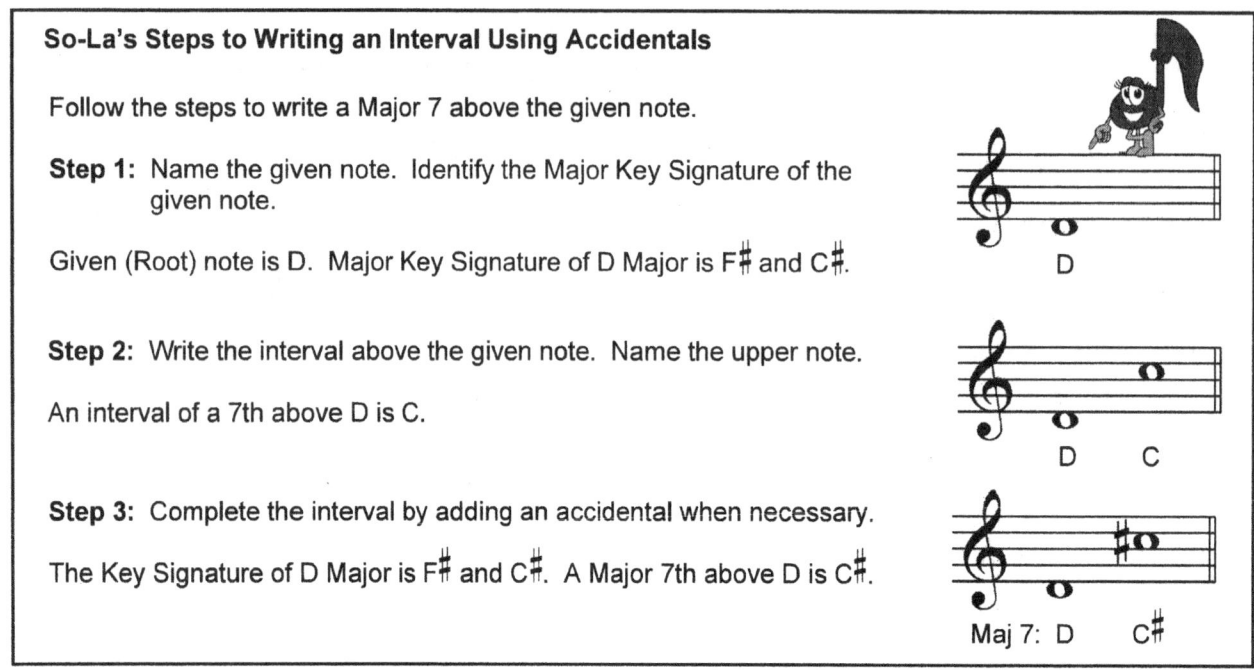

**So-La's Steps to Writing an Interval Using Accidentals**

Follow the steps to write a Major 7 above the given note.

**Step 1:** Name the given note. Identify the Major Key Signature of the given note.

Given (Root) note is D. Major Key Signature of D Major is F♯ and C♯.

**Step 2:** Write the interval above the given note. Name the upper note.

An interval of a 7th above D is C.

**Step 3:** Complete the interval by adding an accidental when necessary.

The Key Signature of D Major is F♯ and C♯. A Major 7th above D is C♯.

♫ **Ti-Do Tip:** If the interval is a minor 3, write the Major 3 first and then lower the upper note one half step (using the same letter name).

1. a) Name the Root note (the given note) of the Interval.
   b) Following "So-La's Steps to Writing an Interval Using Accidentals", write the following melodic intervals. Use whole notes. Name the upper note of the Interval. Complete the interval by adding an accidental when necessary.

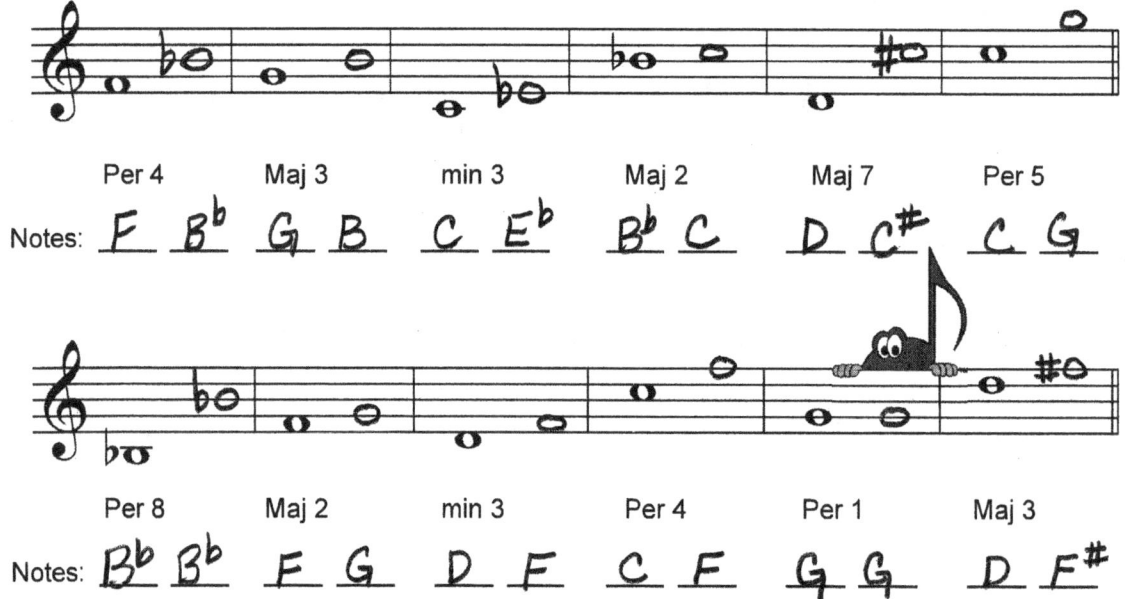

Per 4 — Notes: F B♭
Maj 3 — G B
min 3 — C E♭
Maj 2 — B♭ C
Maj 7 — D C♯
Per 5 — C G

Per 8 — B♭ B♭
Maj 2 — F G
min 3 — D F
Per 4 — C F
Per 1 — G G
Maj 3 — D F♯

# NAMING and WRITING INTERVALS - USING ACCIDENTALS or a KEY SIGNATURE

An interval is two notes - a lower note (the Root note) and the upper (higher) note.
An interval can be written using accidentals or a Key Signature.

> **So-La Says:** An interval can be written as a Harmonic Interval or as a Melodic Interval.
>
> To write a **Harmonic Interval**, the note is written directly above the
> lower note (or touching the lower note for a first or a second).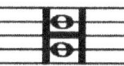
>
> To write a **Melodic Interval**, the note is written beside the lower note
> (at an appropriate distance away from the lower note).

♫ **Ti-Do Tip:** The **size** of the interval is the interval number.
　　　　　　　 The **quality** of the interval is whether it is Major, minor or Perfect.

1. Write the following harmonic intervals above each given note.  Use whole notes.  Use accidentals when necessary.

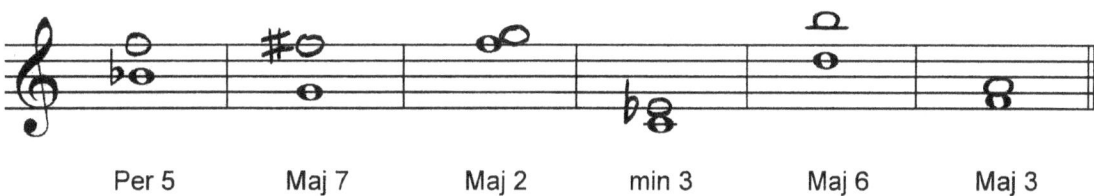

2. Observing the Major Key Signatures, write the following melodic intervals above each given note. Use whole notes.  Use accidentals when necessary.

3. Name the following intervals.

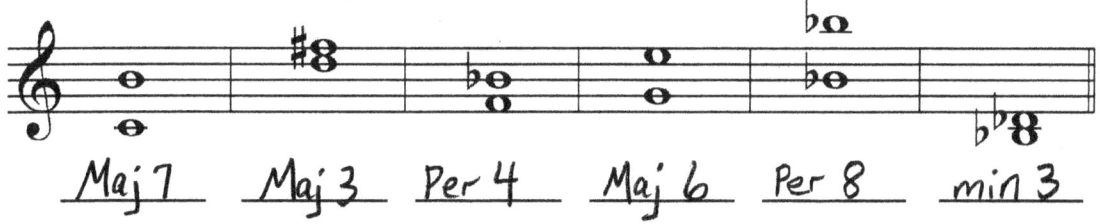

Maj 7   Maj 3   Per 4   Maj 6   Per 8   min 3

>  ♫ **Ti-Do Time:** LISTEN as your Teacher plays the intervals on Pages 26 and 27.
>
> 　　　　　　　Identify if the interval played is a harmonic interval or a melodic interval.
>
> 　　　　　　　Identify the name (size and quality) of each interval.

# TONIC and DOMINANT TRIADS - MAJOR SCALES

The triad built on Scale Degree $\hat{1}$ of the Major scale is called the **Tonic** Triad. It is a Major triad. The Tonic Triad uses the notes of the Major scale.

Tonic Major triad: Root (Tonic $\hat{1}$) - Major 3 (Mediant $\hat{3}$) - Perfect 5 (Dominant $\hat{5}$).

The triad built on Scale Degree $\hat{5}$ of the Major scale is called the **Dominant Triad**. It is a Major triad. The Dominant Triad uses the notes of the Major scale.

Dominant Major triad: Root (Dominant $\hat{5}$) - Major 3 (Leading Tone $\hat{7}$) - Perfect 5 (Supertonic $\hat{2}$).

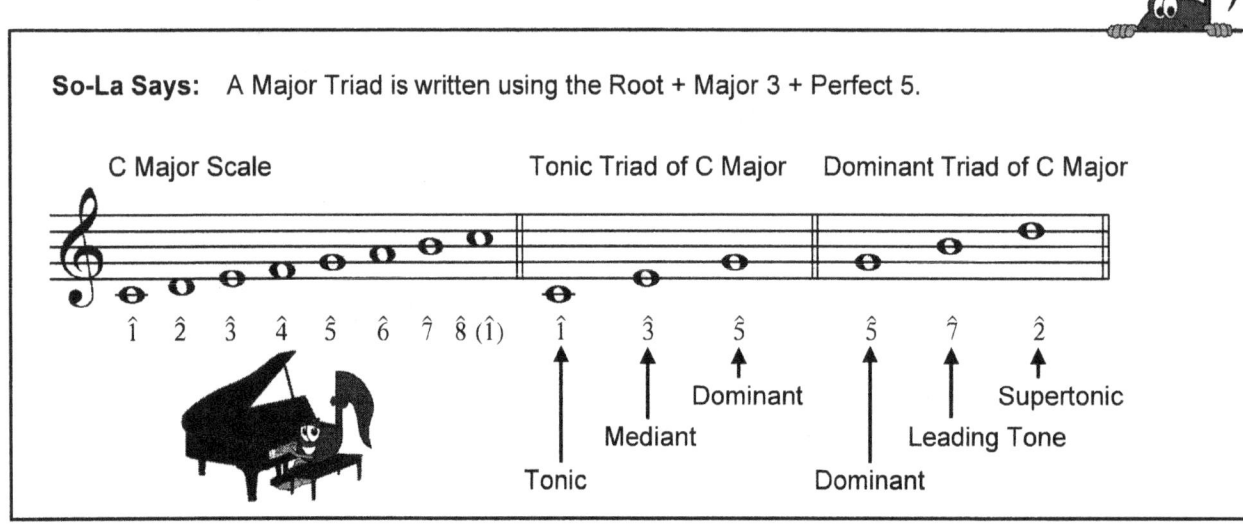

**So-La Says:** A Major Triad is written using the Root + Major 3 + Perfect 5.

1. a) In measure 1, write the Major scale. Use a Key Signature. Use whole notes.
   b) In measure 2, write the Tonic triad, ascending. Use whole notes.
   c) In measure 3, write the Dominant triad, ascending. Use whole notes.

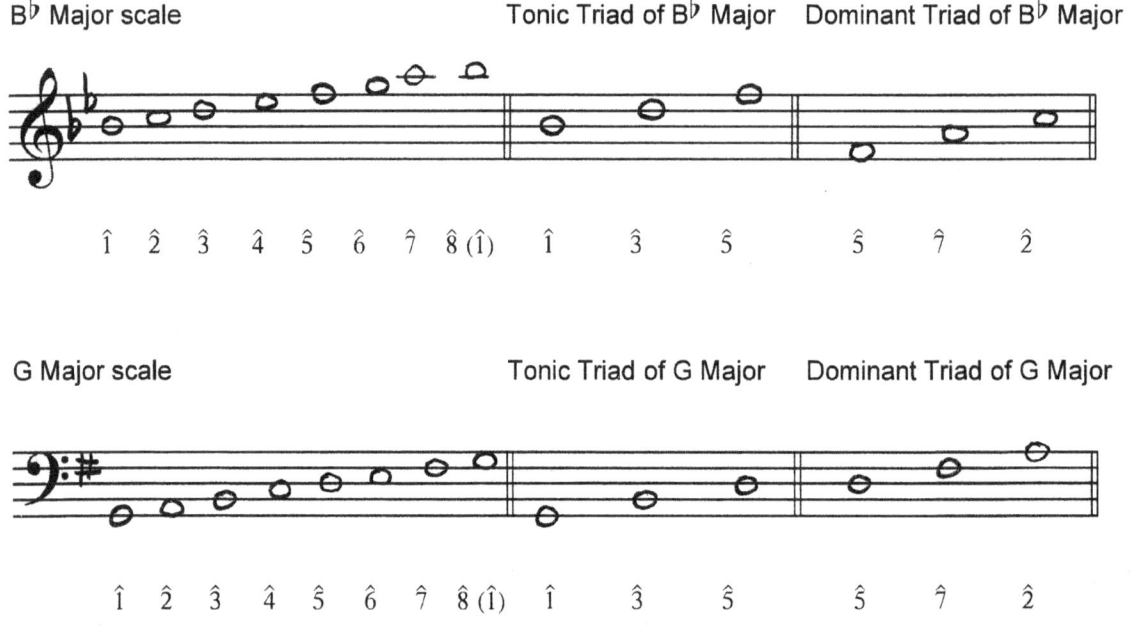

## TONIC and DOMINANT TRIADS - HARMONIC MINOR SCALES

There are 3 forms of minor scales - natural minor, harmonic minor and melodic minor. When identifying the Tonic and Dominant Triads of a minor key, use the notes of the harmonic minor scale.

The triad built on Scale Degree $\hat{1}$ of the harmonic minor scale is called the **Tonic** Triad. It is a minor triad. The Tonic Triad uses the notes of the harmonic minor scale.

Tonic minor triad: Root (Tonic $\hat{1}$) - minor 3 (Mediant $\hat{3}$) - Perfect 5 (Dominant $\hat{5}$).

The triad built on Scale Degree $\hat{5}$ of the harmonic minor scale is called the **Dominant Triad**. It is a Major triad. The Dominant Triad uses the notes of the harmonic minor scale.

Dominant Major triad: Root (Dominant $\hat{5}$) - Major 3 (raised Leading Tone $\hat{7}$) - Perfect 5 (Supertonic $\hat{2}$).

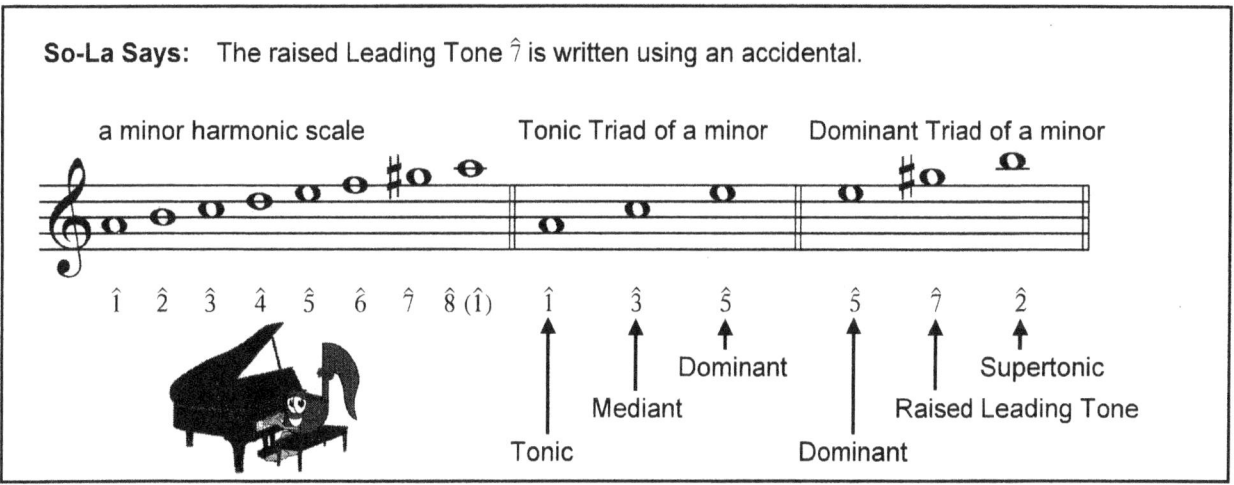

**So-La Says:** The raised Leading Tone $\hat{7}$ is written using an accidental.

1. a) In measure 1, write the harmonic minor scale. Use a Key Signature. Use whole notes.
   b) In measure 2, write the Tonic triad, ascending. Use whole notes.
   c) In measure 3, write the Dominant triad, ascending. Use whole notes.

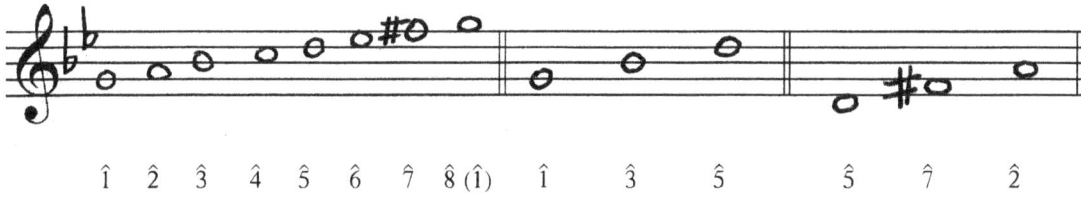

♫ **Ti-Do Time:** LISTEN as your Teacher plays the scales and triads on Pages 28 and 29.

Identify if the scale played is a Major scale or a harmonic minor scale.

Identify if the triad played is a Major triad or a minor triad.

## TONIC and DOMINANT FUNCTIONAL CHORD SYMBOLS - MAJOR SCALES

The triad built on Scale Degree $\hat{1}$ of the Major scale is called the **Tonic** Triad. It is a Major triad. The **Functional Chord Symbol** for the Tonic Triad is I.

The triad built on Scale Degree $\hat{5}$ of the Major scale is called the **Dominant Triad**. It is a Major triad. The **Functional Chord Symbol** for the Dominant Triad is V.

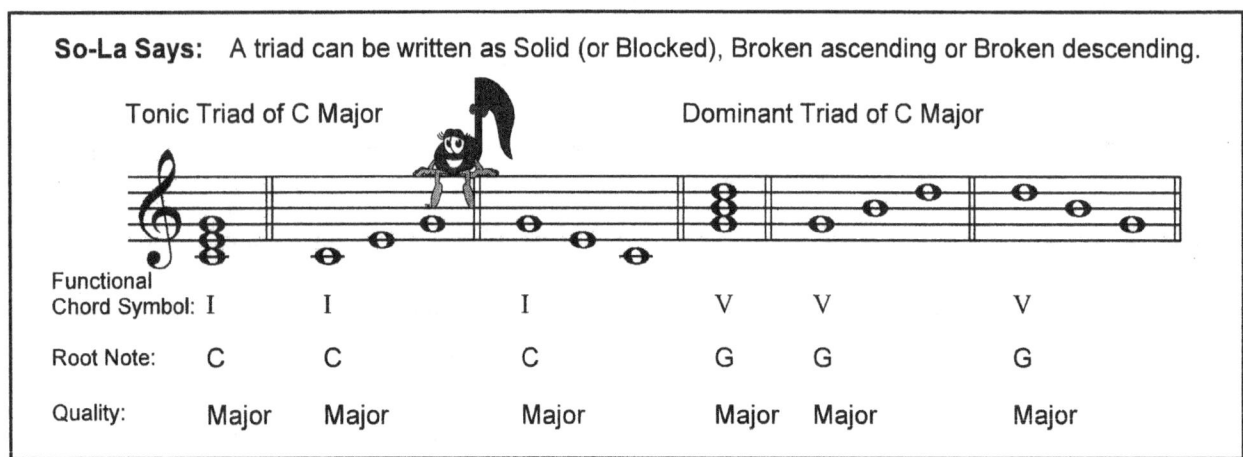

**So-La Says:** A triad can be written as Solid (or Blocked), Broken ascending or Broken descending.

♪ **Ti-Do Tip:** The Functional Chord Symbol is written below the first note of the broken triad.

1. The following triads are written in the key of B♭ Major.
    a) Identify the Root Note and the Quality (Major or minor) of each Triad.
    b) Identify a Tonic Triad with the Functional Chord Symbol I and a Dominant Triad with the Functional Chord Symbol V.

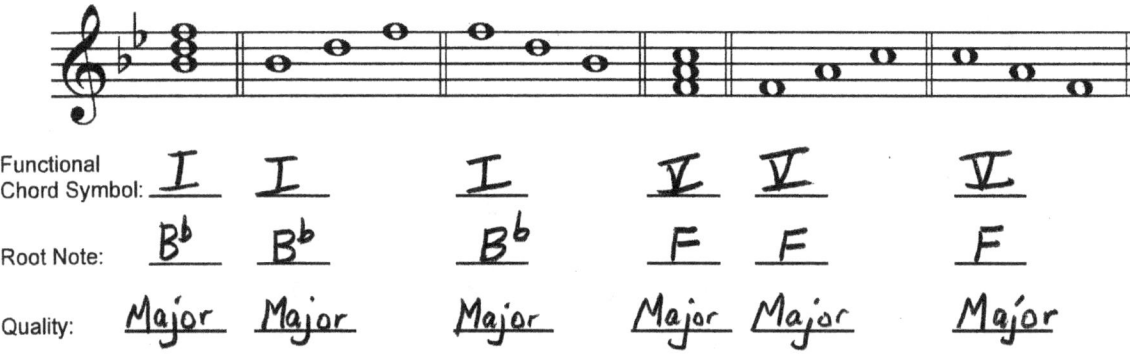

2. a) Name the Major key.
   b) Identify the Functional Chord Symbol for each triad.

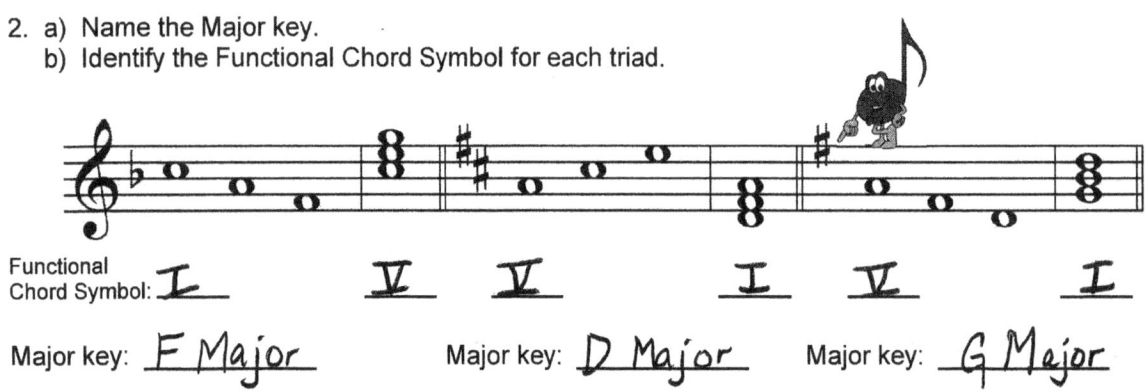

# TONIC and DOMINANT FUNCTIONAL CHORD SYMBOLS - MINOR SCALES

The triad built on Scale Degree $\hat{1}$ of the harmonic minor scale is called the **Tonic** Triad. It is a minor triad. The **Functional Chord Symbol** for the Tonic Triad is i.

The triad built on Scale Degree $\hat{5}$ of the harmonic minor scale is called the **Dominant Triad**. It is a Major triad. The **Functional Chord Symbol** for the Dominant Triad is V.

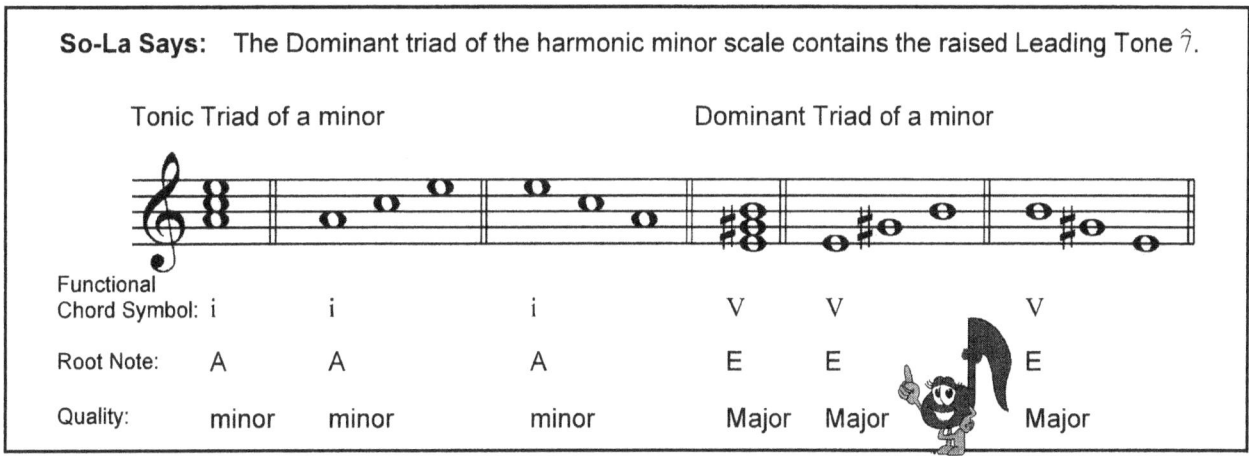

♪ **Ti-Do Tip:** A Major triad uses an upper case Roman Numeral. A minor triad uses a lower case.

1. The following triads are written in the key of g minor.
   a) Identify the Root Note and the Quality (Major or minor) of each Triad.
   b) Identify a Tonic Triad with the Functional Chord Symbol i and a Dominant Triad with the Functional Chord Symbol V.

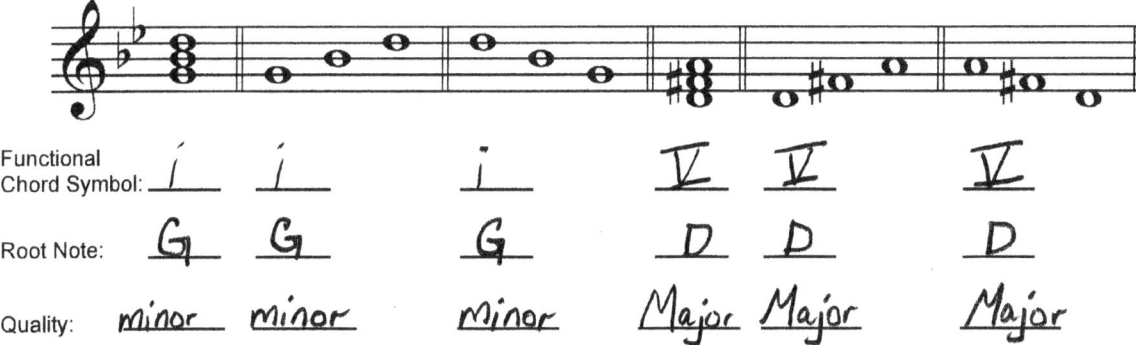

2. a) Name the minor key.
   b) Identify the Functional Chord Symbol for each triad.

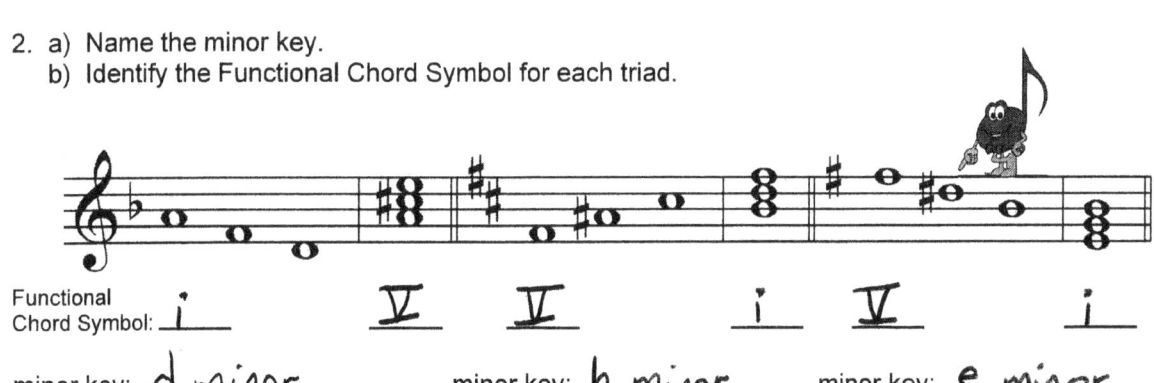

# FUNCTIONAL CHORD SYMBOLS and ROOT/QUALITY CHORD SYMBOLS - TONIC and DOMINANT - MAJOR KEYS

**Root/Quality Chord Symbols** are Letter Names that indicate the quality (Major or minor) of a triad.

An Upper Case letter indicates a Major triad. (Example: D = D Major triad)
An Upper Case letter with an "m" after it indicates a minor triad. (Example: Dm = d minor triad)

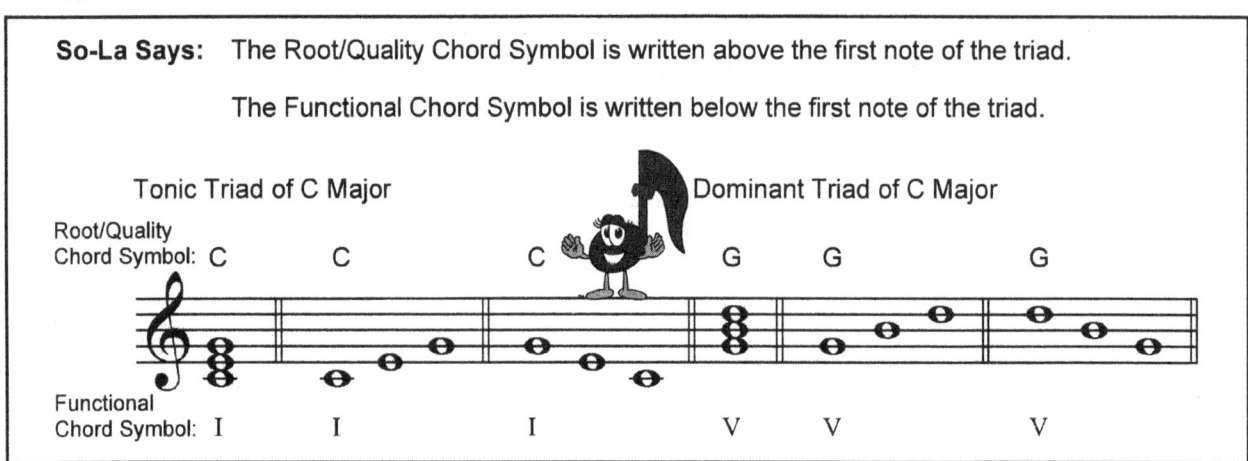

♪ **Ti-Do Tip:** The Tonic Triad of a Major key is a Major triad.
   The Dominant Triad of a Major key is a Major triad.

1. The following triads are written in the key of D Major.
   a) Write the Root/Quality Chord Symbol above each triad.
   b) Write the Functional Chord Symbol below each triad.

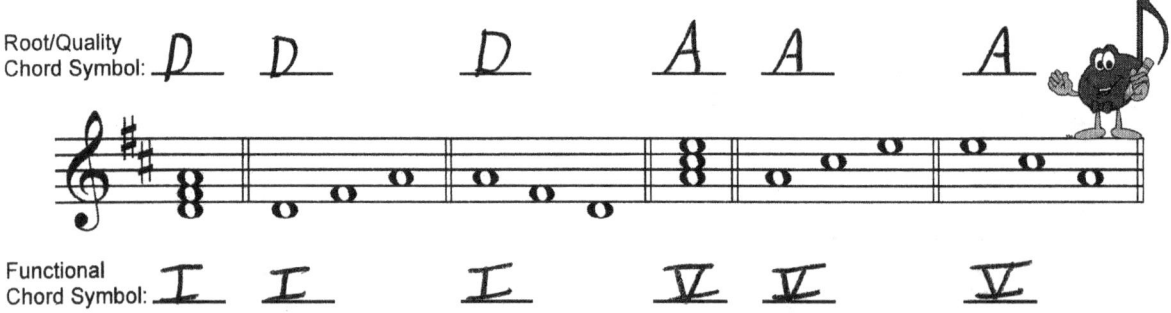

2. a) Name the Major key.
   b) Write the Root/Quality Chord Symbol above each triad.
   c) Write the Functional Chord Symbol below each triad.

# FUNCTIONAL CHORD SYMBOLS and ROOT/QUALITY CHORD SYMBOLS - TONIC and DOMINANT - MINOR KEYS

**Root/Quality Chord Symbols** are Letter Names that indicate the quality (Major or minor) of a triad.

An Upper Case letter indicates a Major triad. (Example: G = G Major triad)
An Upper Case letter with an "m" after it indicates a minor triad. (Example: Gm = g minor triad)

**So-La Says:** The Root/Quality Chord Symbol is written above the first note of the triad.

The Functional Chord Symbol is written below the first note of the triad.

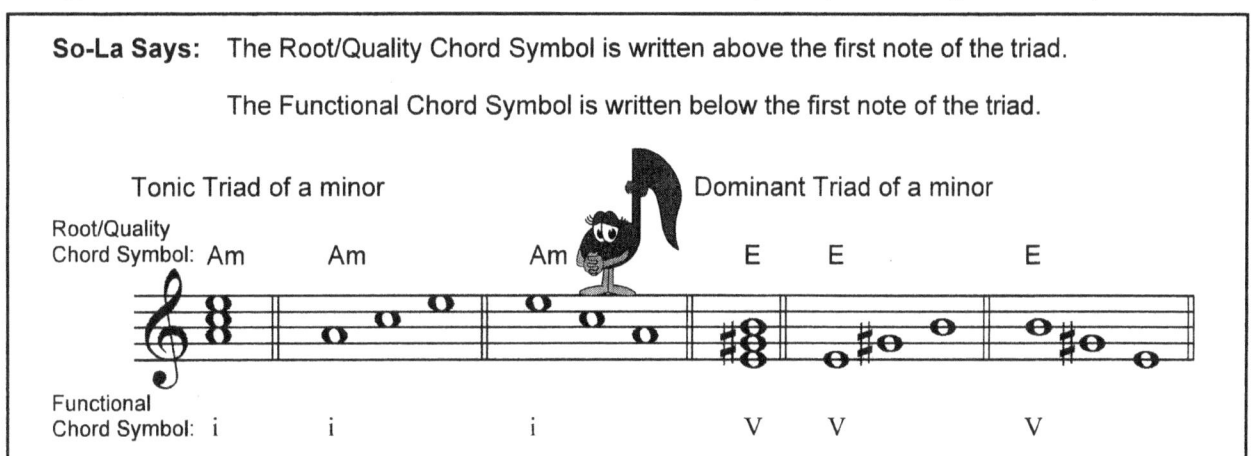

♫ **Ti-Do Tip:** Using the notes of the harmonic minor scale, the Tonic Triad of a minor key is a minor triad and the Dominant Triad of a minor key is a Major triad.

1. The following triads are written in the key of b minor.
   a) Write the Root/Quality Chord Symbol above each triad.
   b) Write the Functional Chord Symbol below each triad.

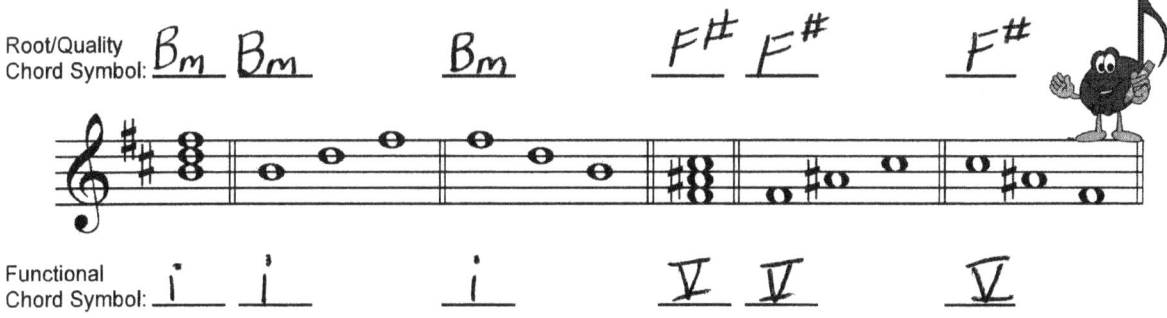

2. a) Name the minor key.
   b) Write the Root/Quality Chord Symbol above each triad.
   c) Write the Functional Chord Symbol below each triad.

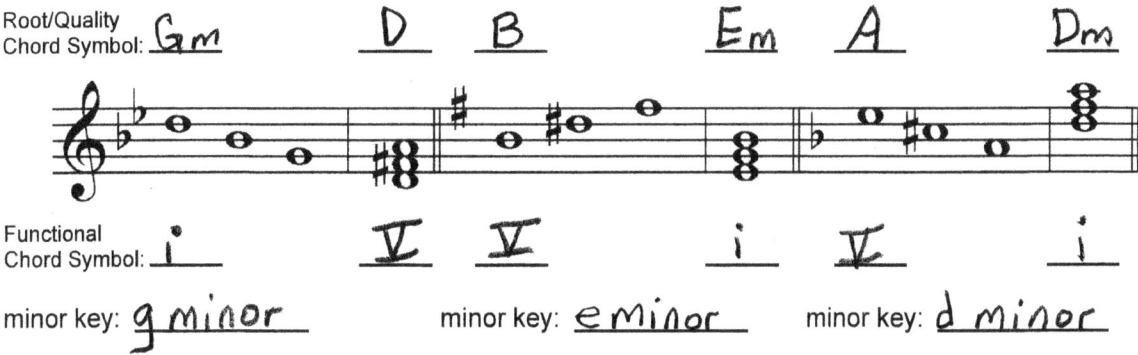

# WRITING TONIC and DOMINANT TRIADS - MAJOR and MINOR KEYS

1. Write the solid (blocked) triad indicated by the Root/Quality Chord Symbol. Use whole notes. Use the correct Key Signature and any necessary accidentals.

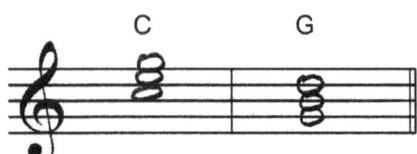

Major key: C Major

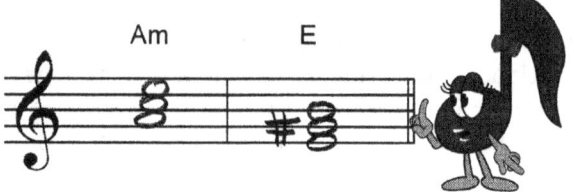

Relative minor key: a minor

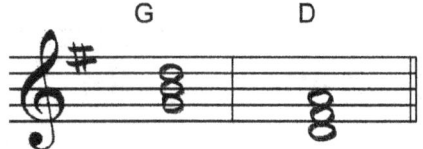

Major key: G Major

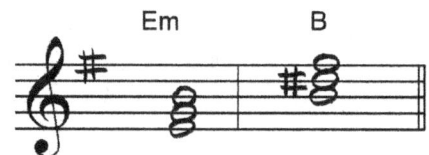

Relative minor key: e minor

Major key: D Major

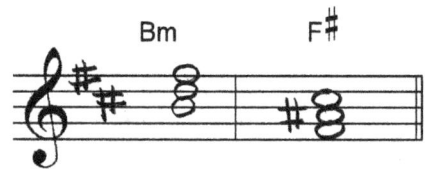

Relative minor key: b minor

Major key: F Major

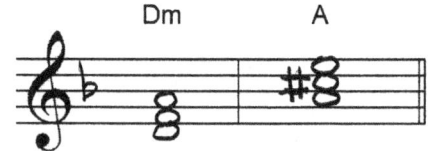

Relative minor key: d minor

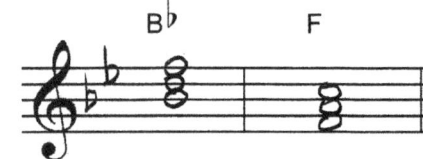

Major key: B♭ Major

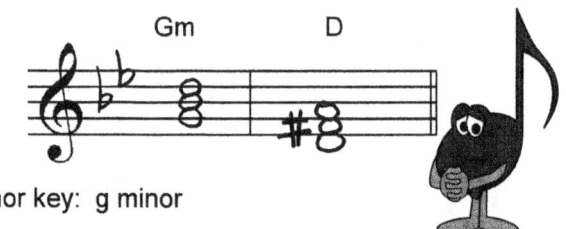

Relative minor key: g minor

# MUSIC TERMS and SIGNS

**OTTAVA**, or $8^{va}$, is the interval of an octave.

$8^{va}{-}{-}{-}{-}{-}\rceil$  Indicates to play the notes **one octave higher** than written.

$8^{va}{-}{-}{-}{-}{-}\rfloor$  Indicates to play the notes **one octave lower** than written.

1. Draw a line from each note on the staff to the corresponding key on the keyboard (at the correct pitch). Name the key directly on the keyboard.

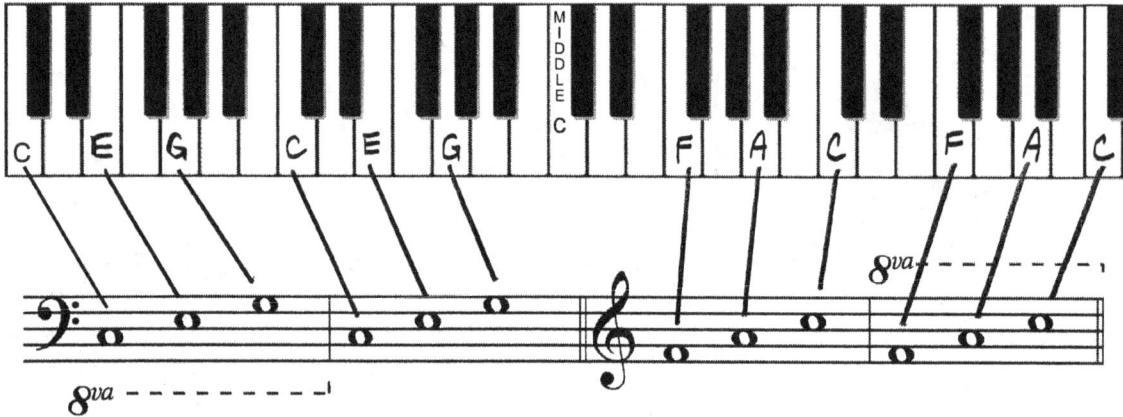

**So-La Says:** Musical Terms can be used to indicate Style in Performance.

*cantabile* means in a singing style.

*dolce* means sweet, gentle.

*grazioso* means graceful.

*maestoso* means majestic.

*marcato* means marked or stressed.

2. Draw a line to match the Musical Term or Sign with the correct definition.

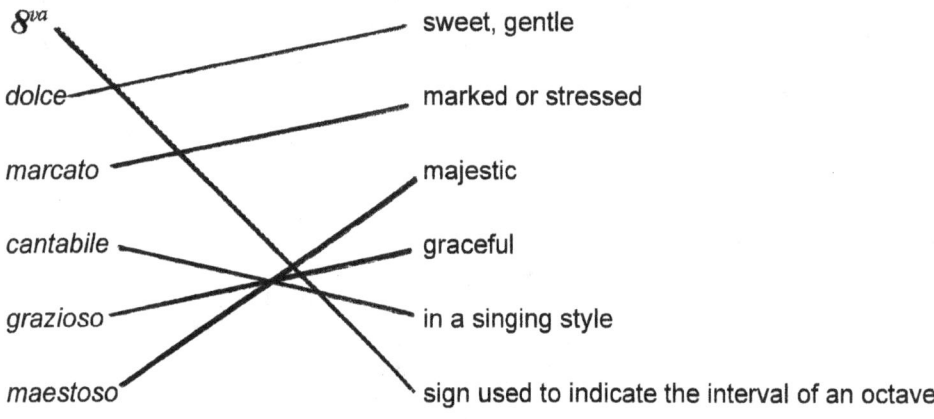

# MELODY TRANSPOSITION - UP or DOWN ONE OCTAVE

A melody may be transposed. Transposing means playing or writing music at a different pitch from the original by raising or lowering all the notes by the same interval.

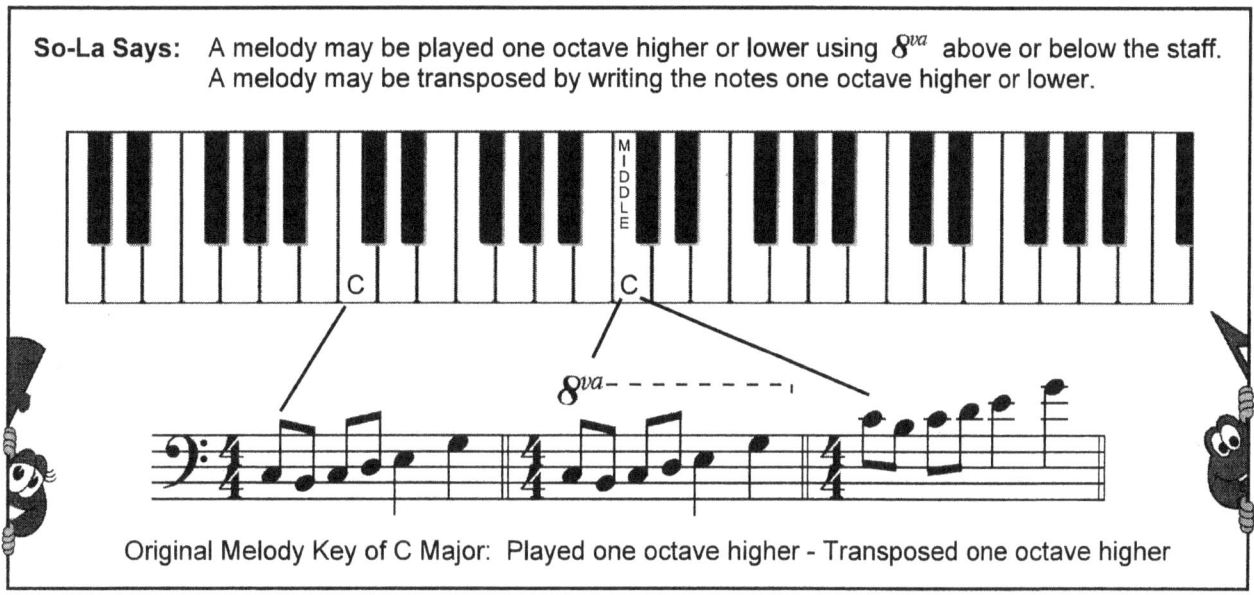

♪ **Ti-Do Tip:** Write the Clef sign, Key Signature and Time Signature. Use appropriate stem directions.

1. Name the Major key. Transpose the melody up one octave in the Bass Clef.

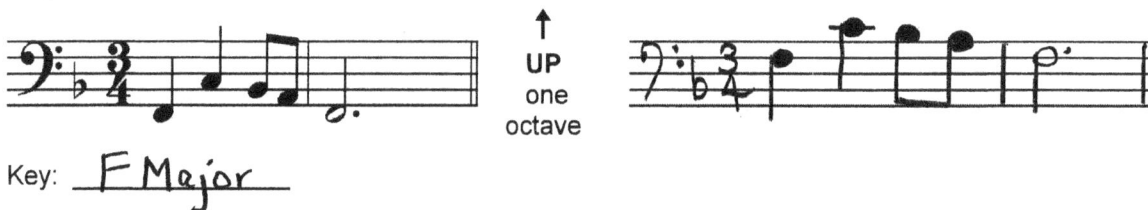

Key: __F Major__

2. Name the Major key. Transpose the melody down one octave in the Bass Clef.

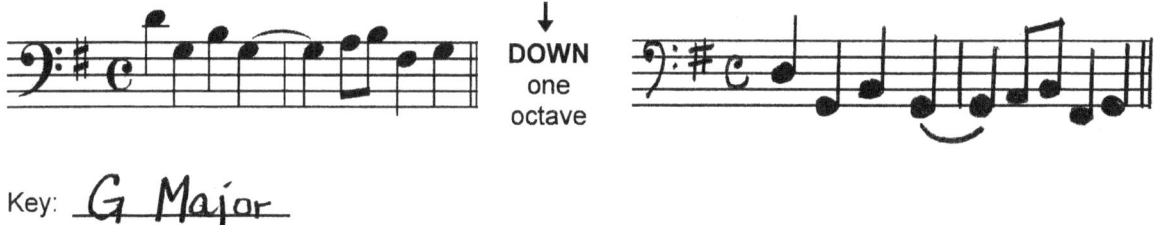

Key: __G Major__

3. Name the Major key. Transpose the melody down one octave in the Treble Clef.

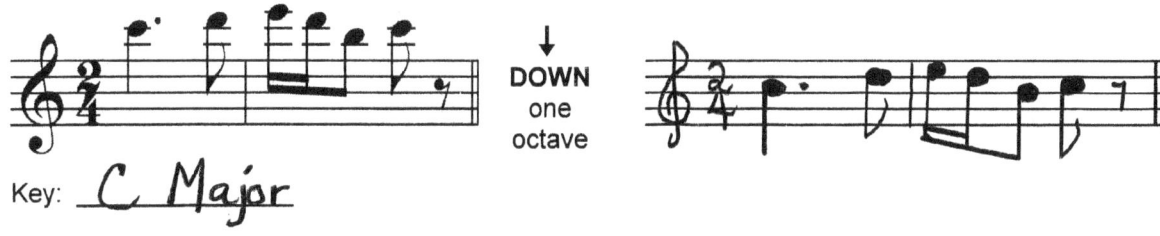

Key: __C Major__

# ANALYSIS of MELODY - MELODIC PHRASES (SAME, SIMILAR OR DIFFERENT)

A melody has a motive (short musical idea) which may be repeated or altered to create a melodic phrase (musical sentence). A melodic phrase may be 2 - 4 measures or more.

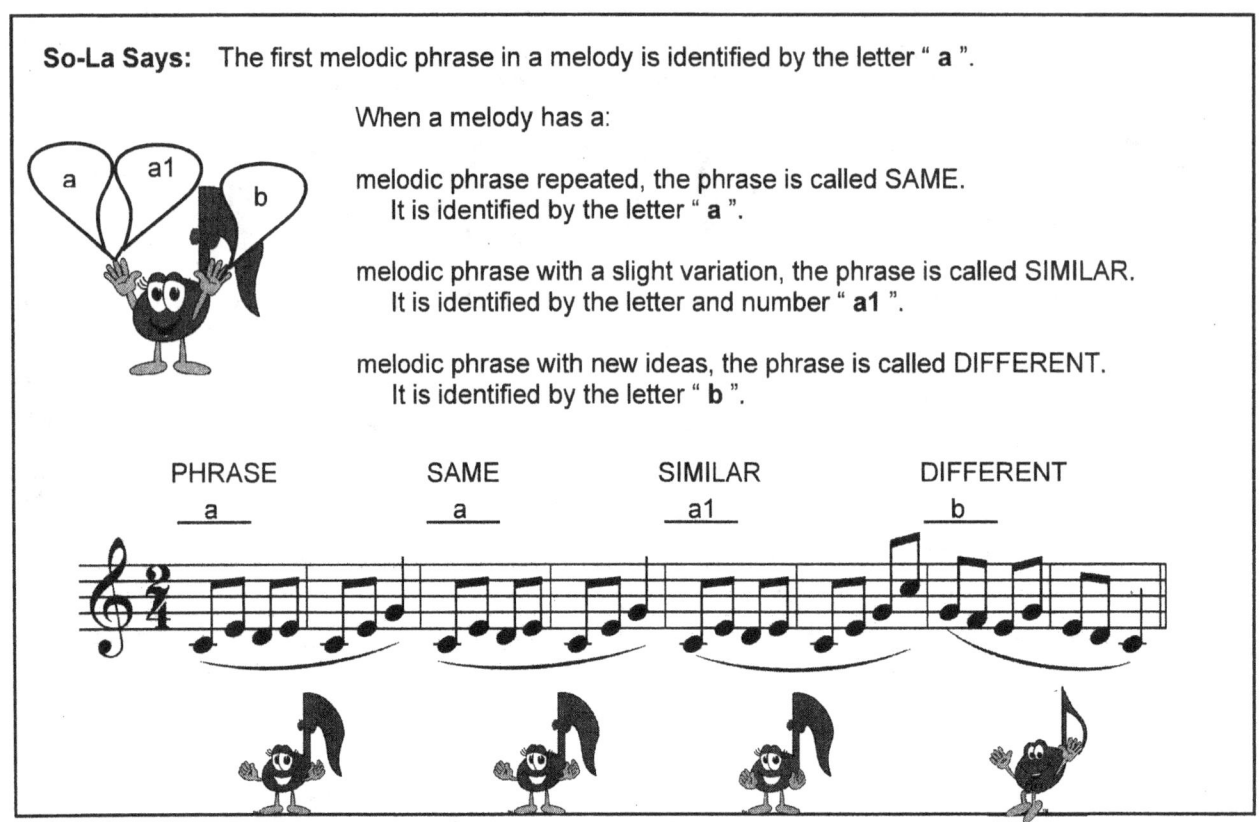

♫ **Ti-Do Tip:** A melody may repeat the same phrase (a), or have a similar phrase (a1), or have a different phrase (b) that creates a series of melodic phrases within a piece of music.

1. Identify each of the melodic phrases directly above each phrase as: a, a1, or b.

# MELODY WRITING - LEAPS BETWEEN NOTES of the TONIC and DOMINANT TRIADS

A melody may use repeated notes (interval of a first), notes moving by step (interval of a second), a skip (interval of a third), or a leap (interval larger than a third such as an interval of a fourth or a fifth).

A melody may be written using leaps of notes within a triad. In the key of G Major, using the notes within the Tonic triad, moving from G to D is an interval of a fifth (leap).

1. This melody is in the key of G Major and uses steps, skips and leaps (using notes within the Tonic triad of G Major). The melody ends on stable degree $\hat{1}$.

   a) Circle all the intervals of a fifth (leap) using notes from the Tonic triad of G Major.

   b) Circle if the triad in measure 2 is the: (Tonic triad) or Dominant triad.

   c) Circle if the melodic pattern in measure 1 and in measure 3 is the: same or (similar) or different.

   d) Circle the number of intervals of a third (skip) played in this melody: (2) or 3 or 5.

In the key of C Major, moving from the Tonic note C down to the Dominant note G is an interval of a fourth (leap). Using notes within the Dominant triad, moving from G up to D is an interval of a fifth (leap).

2. This melody is in the key of C Major and uses steps, skips and leaps (using notes within the Tonic Triad and within the Dominant triad of C Major). The melody ends on stable degree $\hat{3}$.

   a) Circle all the intervals of a fifth (leap) using notes from the Dominant triad of C Major.

   b) Circle if the descending triad in measure 2 is the: Tonic triad or (Dominant triad).

   c) Circle if the rhythmic pattern in measure 1 and in measure 2 is the: (same) or similar or different.

   d) Circle the number of intervals of a fourth (leap) played in this melody: 2 or (3) or 5.

♫ **Ti-Do Tip:** Play the above melodies on your instrument. Listen for steps, skips and leaps.

# MELODY WRITING - ENDING on STABLE SCALE DEGREES

A melody ending on the Tonic note (stable degree $\hat{1}$) or ending on the Mediant note (stable degree $\hat{3}$) sounds finished and complete (like a musical period at the end of a musical sentence).

The notes from the Tonic and the Dominant triads provide the foundation for the melody. Non-triad notes can be used as "Passing Tones" - notes that move by step to connect the notes of the triads.

1. Compose three melodies below. Use the given rhythm.
   a) Name the Major key. Name the notes of the Tonic and the Dominant triads.
   b) Use notes moving by step, skip or leap (using notes within the Tonic or Dominant triads).
   c) End on a stable degree. Label the final note as stable degree $\hat{1}$ or $\hat{3}$.
   d) Draw a double bar line at the end. Perform your compositions for family and friends!

# ANALYSIS and MELODY WRITING - MOTIVE AND PHRASE

To create a phrase, a melody may have a repeated **motive pattern** identified as repetition, rhythmic and/or melodic. A melody may have a repeated **melodic phrase** identified as same (a), similar (a1) or different (b). A **phrase** may end on an unstable scale degree ($\hat{2}$ or $\hat{7}$). A **melody** should end on a stable degree ($\hat{1}$ or $\hat{3}$).

1. Analyze the music in C Major by answering the questions below.

a) Circle if the repeated motive pattern in measure 2 is: repetition or (rhythmic) or melodic.

b) Circle if the rhythmic pattern in measure 3 and measure 4 is the: same or (different).

c) Circle if the phrase ending in measure 4 is: a stable scale degree or (an unstable scale degree).

d) Circle if the first phrase (a) and second phrase are: same (a) or (similar (a1)) or different (b).

e) Circle if the phrase ending in measure 8 is: (a stable scale degree) or an unstable scale degree.

f) Compose a melody in measures 10, 11 and 12. Use the given rhythm. Use notes moving by step, skip or leap. End on a stable scale degree.

g) Add a phrase marking above measures 9 to 12.

♫ **Ti-Do Tip:** Play the music on your instrument.

# IMAGINE, COMPOSE, EXPLORE

**Composing** means to create music. Use the composing techniques you have learned to compose your own music. Perform your composition for your friends.

♪ Imagine the music telling a story or an idea. The title (written at the top) describes the composition.
♪ Compose your musical idea. The name (written at the top right) identifies the composer.
♪ Explore the music. Add "So-La Sparkles" using dynamics and articulation to enhance the sound.

---

**So-La Says:** First compose freely without writing anything down. Use a recording device to record your composition. Be creative!

Use the recording to assist you in writing out your composition. Use different dynamics, articulation and tempo to create different sounds and adventures.

---

1. For each of the following: compose a melody in measures 2, 3 and 4. Use your own rhythm.

    a) Imagine your musical idea by completing the title at the top. Write your name as the composer.
    b) Compose a melody in the given Key Signature and Time Signature. End on the Tonic $\hat{1}$ note.
    c) Explore the music. Add "So-La Sparkles" using dynamics, articulation, terms, $8^{va}$, etc.

(one possible answer)

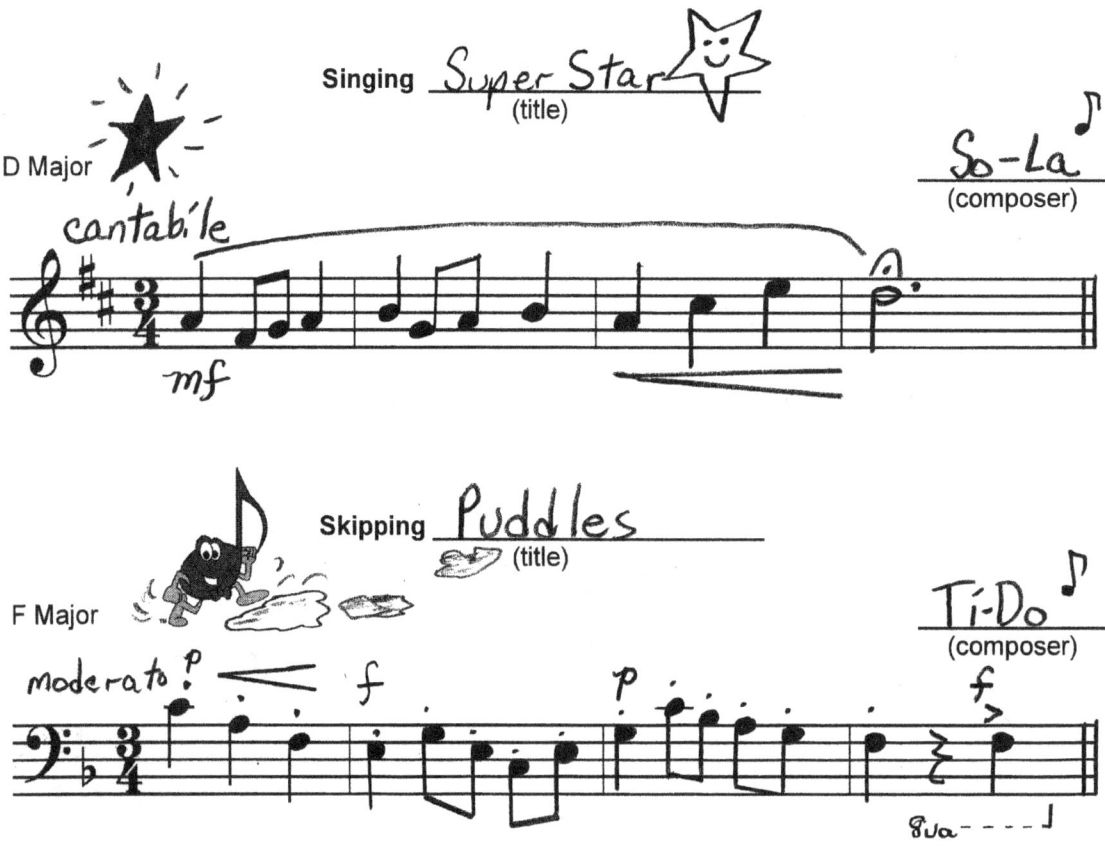

## ANALYSIS and SIGHT READING

**Little Hamster**

Julianne Warkentin

1. Analyze the music by answering the questions below.  Play (Sight Read) the piece "Little Hamster".

   a) Name the key. __g minor__   Explain the F sharp in measure 4. __raised 7th note__

   b) Circle if the first phrase (mm. 1 - 4) and second phrase (mm. 5 - 8) are:   same (a)   or   (different (b)).

   c) Explain the sign at the letter A. __Play the notes one octave higher__

   d) Explain the sign at the letter B. __Slowing down__

   e) Circle if the triad at the letter C is the:   Tonic triad   or   (Dominant triad).

   f) Circle if the first phrase (mm. 1 - 4) and third phrase (mm. 9 - 12) are:   same (a)   or   (similar (a1)).

   g) Explain the sign at the letter D. __return to original tempo__

   h) Circle the number of phrases that are in the piece "Little Hamster":   (three)   or   twelve.

# MUSIC HISTORY - JOHANN SEBASTIAN BACH (1685 - 1750)

**Johann Sebastian Bach** (the youngest of eight children) was born in Eisenach, Germany on March 21, 1685. His family was very musical, and many of his relatives were professional musicians. J.S. Bach studied stringed instruments with his father, a court trumpeter, until he was orphaned at the age of ten. His oldest brother Johann Christoph, an organist, took him in and taught him the harpsichord and the organ.

J.S. Bach became a professional musician at the age of 15. He was hired as a singer in the choir at St. Michael's Lutheran Church in Lundeberg.

When Bach's voice changed, he then focused on the violin and harpsichord. He became an accomplished performer and the greatest organist of his time.

Bach composed many musical works and his logical mind was interested in organizing ideas into the proper form (such as the Baroque Suite).

J.S. Bach is one of the most famous composers of the Baroque Period (1600 - 1750). Bach wrote many Baroque Suites - a series of dances that include the Gavotte and Gigue.

Bach had 20 children!

Bach had 7 children with his first wife Maria Barbara (married in 1707). Two of their sons, Wilhelm Friedemann and Carl Philipp Emanuel, became great composers.

Bach had 13 children with his second wife Anna Magdalena Wilcke (married in 1721). Two of their sons, Johann Christoph Friedrich and Johann Christian, became great composers too.

Bach wrote many teaching pieces for his children and students: 20 little preludes for keyboard, suites based on dance forms, inventions, 24 preludes and fugues in "The Well-tempered Clavier" and more.

1. Check (✓) the correct answer.

   a) What year was J.S. Bach born? — ✓ 1685 or ☐ 1750

   b) What instrument did Bach excel at playing? — ☐ trumpet or ✓ organ

   c) What musical period is Bach from? — ☐ Romantic or ✓ Baroque

   d) How many of Bach's sons were great composers? — ✓ four or ☐ ten

   e) What country did Bach live in? — ☐ France or ✓ Germany

# MUSIC HISTORY - THE ANNA MAGDALENA NOTEBOOK

Bach gave his wife Anna Magdalena two handwritten notebooks (one in 1722 and the other larger notebook in 1725) in which to write music. They're known as the *Anna Magdalena Notebook* - a collection of dances, arias, chorales and other pieces composed by Bach, Carl Phillip Emmanuel, Christian Petzold and others.

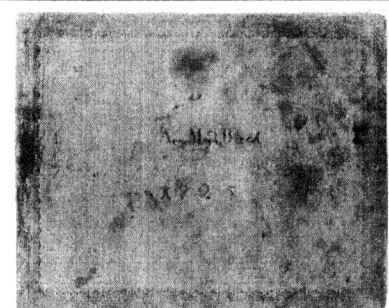

The notebook had a beautiful green cover and included Anna Magdalena Bach's initials *AMB* and the year 1725 written in gold. The pages had gold gilt edging and vellum covered binding.

The first piece in the notebook is the Partita BWV 827 in A minor, or AM - the initials of Anna Magdalena (a singer and musician).

Many of the 42 Baroque pieces (written for harpsichord) were entered in the notebook by Anna Magdalena herself.

The Baroque era was one of extravagance, luxury and overindulgence. The music was decorative and ornate, as was the architecture, clothing, hair styles, art work, etc.

The music had a sense of splendor with melody lines in decorative Major/minor tonalities, rhythmic energy, meter (duple, triple or quadruple), various tempos, abrupt dynamic shifts and polyphonic texture (two or more independent melodic lines). Baroque Dance Forms include the Menuet, Gavotte and Gigue.

1. Fill in the blanks using the following terms to complete the elements of music in the Baroque era.

    Melody, Rhythm, Meter, Tempo, Dynamics, Polyphonic, Dances

a) A Major or minor tonality with a single melodic idea is called the __melody__.

b) The patterns, organization and combination of notes and rests is called the __rhythm__.

c) The Time Signature indicates the pulse or rhythmic emphasis and is called the __meter__.

d) The speed at which the pulses or units of meter are played is called the __tempo__.

e) The abrupt shifts and changes from loud to soft or soft to loud are called the __dynamics__.

f) Two or more independent melodic lines played at the same time is called __polyphonic__ texture.

g) The Menuet, Gavotte and Gigue are pieces written in the form of Baroque __dances__.

## MUSIC HISTORY - MUSIC FOR DANCING and the HARPSICHORD

In the Baroque Period, **Music for Dancing** was often performed on the keyboard/harpsichord. A collection of Baroque Dances, all in one key, was called a Suite.

A Baroque Suite contains four standard movements: Allemande, Courante, Sarabande and Gigue. Other Baroque dances include the Bourrée, Menuet (also called Minuet) and Gavotte.

**Baroque Dances:** (Duple meter - group of 2; Triple meter - group of 3; Quadruple meter - group of 4)

- Allemande - Graceful German dance in moderately fast duple meter.
- Courante - Serious French dance in slow triple meter with complicated duple/triple rhythms.
- Sarabande - Elegant Spanish dance in slow triple meter, emphasis on the 2nd beat of the measure.
- Gigue - Lively English origin dance in fast meter (6/8, 9/8, 12/8 or 12/16), with a short upbeat.
- Bourrée - Vigorous French dance in strong rhythmic 4/4 or 2/2 time, begins with an upbeat.
- Menuet - Minuet, Formal French dance (small steps) in moderate triple meter (*tempo di minuetto*).
- Gavotte - Sentimental French dance in moderate duple/quadruple meter (*tempo di gavotta*), begins with a half-measure upbeat or anacrusis.

1. Fill in the blanks with the correct names of the Baroque Dances.

   a) __Menuet__ - Formal French dance in moderately fast 3/4 time, with dainty small dance steps.

   b) __Gavotte__ - Sentimental French dance in moderate duple/quadruple meter, begins with a half-measure upbeat or anacrusis.

   c) __Gigue__ - Lively English origin dance in fast meter (6/8, 9/8, 12/8 or 12/16), with a short upbeat.

**The Harpsichord** was played as a solo keyboard instrument or with a small group of instruments.

The Harpsichord is a keyboard instrument (with 4 - 6 octaves) similar to a piano (7 octaves + a min 3). The sound is based on quills that pluck the strings when keys were pressed down.

The sound of a note could not be sustained. A trill (a symbol of a musical ornament indicating a rapid alternation between adjacent notes) was placed over a note to extend the sound.

The harpsichord was not capable of producing variations in volume (crescendo and decrescendo).

Harpsichords had one or two (or more) keyboards and various stops to alter a sudden contrast of volume (from soft to loud or loud to soft). These were called terraced dynamics.

2. The keyboard instrument whose quills pluck the strings is called the __harpsichord__.
3. The contrasting dynamics of the Harpsichord is called __terraced dynamics__.
4. The symbol placed over notes to extend the sound is called a __trill (ornament)__.

Go to **GSGMUSIC.com** - Watch Free Resources to learn more about Baroque Dances and the Harpsichord.

# MUSIC APPRECIATION - MENUET in G MAJOR, BWV Anh. 114 by CHRISTIAN PETZOLD

Christian Petzold (1677 - 1733) was a German organist, composer and teacher. His composition of the Menuet in G Major, BWV Anh. 114 is included in the Notebook for Anna Magdalena Bach.

> Baroque music written for the harpsichord featured ornamentation signs to indicate melodic decoration. The shape or symbol indicates how the ornament (embellishment) is to be played.
>
> *tr* or ∿ = Trill (minimum of 4 notes beginning on the upper note, may be a long or short trill)
>
> ∿ = Mordent (the ornamental notes are played as quickly as possible)
>
> ♪ = Appoggiatura (play the small note on the beat followed by the next note)

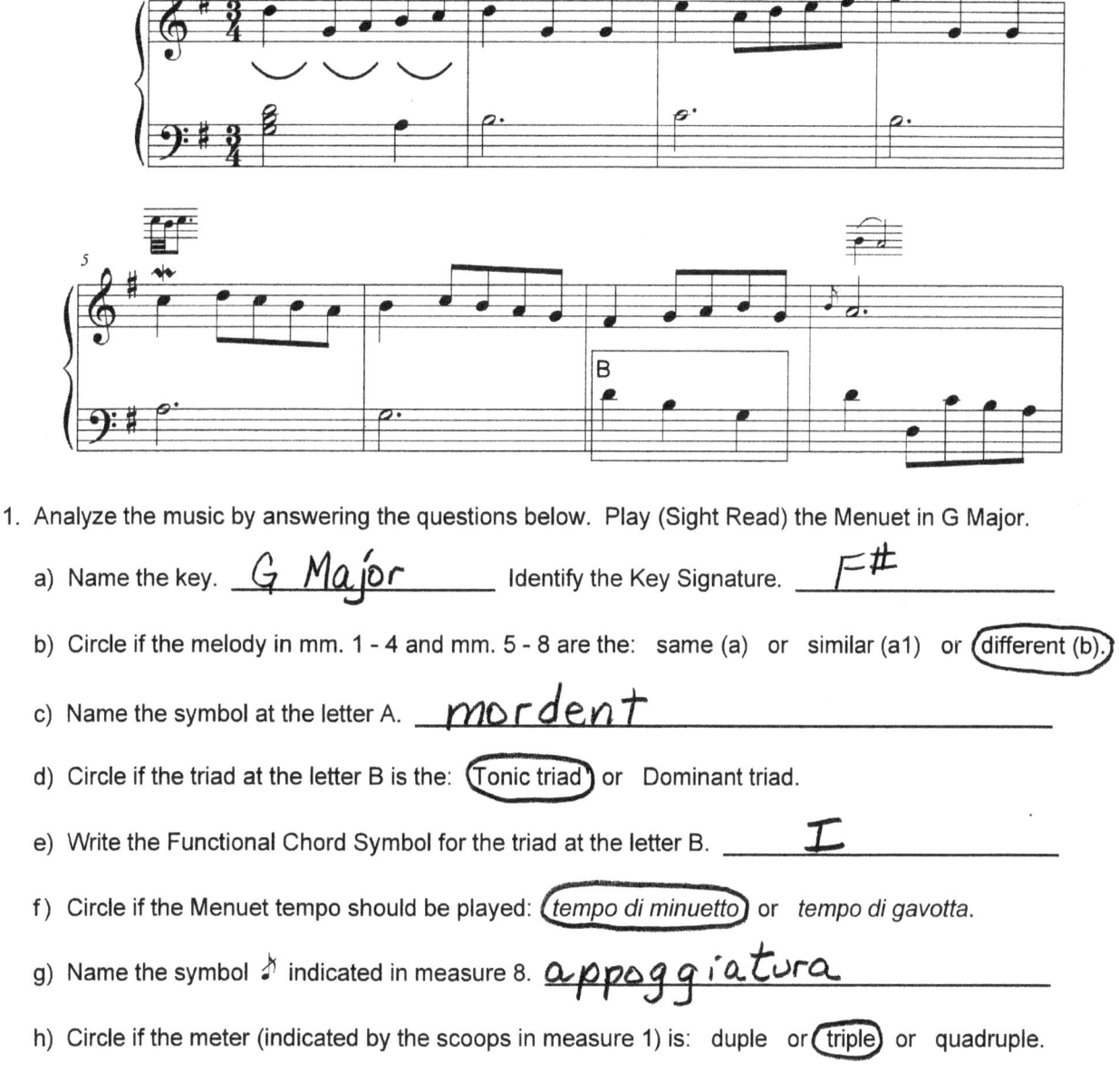

1. Analyze the music by answering the questions below. Play (Sight Read) the Menuet in G Major.

   a) Name the key. __G Major__  Identify the Key Signature. __F#__

   b) Circle if the melody in mm. 1 - 4 and mm. 5 - 8 are the: same (a)  or  similar (a1)  or  **(different (b))**

   c) Name the symbol at the letter A. __mordent__

   d) Circle if the triad at the letter B is the: **(Tonic triad)** or Dominant triad.

   e) Write the Functional Chord Symbol for the triad at the letter B. __I__

   f) Circle if the Menuet tempo should be played: **(tempo di minuetto)** or *tempo di gavotta*.

   g) Name the symbol ♪ indicated in measure 8. __appoggiatura__

   h) Circle if the meter (indicated by the scoops in measure 1) is: duple  or  **(triple)**  or  quadruple.

Go to **GSGMUSIC.com** - For Easy Access to watch videos on the music and dance of the Menuet (Minuet).

**MUSIC APPRECIATION - FRENCH SUITE No. 5 in G MAJOR, BWV 816 GAVOTTE by J.S. BACH**

This Gavotte is from the French Suite No. 5 in G Major by J.S. Bach. This Suite includes the Allemande, Courante, Sarabande, Gavotte, Bourrée, Loure and Gigue (1722 Notebook for Anna Magdalena Bach).

> The Gavotte begins with a two quarter note Upbeat - an Anacrusis (pickup beat). First + last incomplete measures = one complete measure. The Downbeat is the first strong beat in a measure.
>
> 𝄴 is the symbol for $\frac{4}{4}$ time, also called Common Time (4 beats per measure, quarter note = 1 count).
>
> 𝄵 is the symbol for $\frac{2}{2}$ time, also called Cut Time or *alla breve* (2 beats per measure, half note = 1 count).

Gavotte from the French Suite No. 5 in G Major, BWV 816 — J.S. Bach

1. Analyze the music by answering the questions below.

    a) Identify the Time Signature. __𝄵__  There are __2__ beats per measure, __half__ note = 1 count.

    b) Circle if the melody begins on: (an upbeat) or a downbeat.

    c) Explain the symbol at the letter A. __Cut time = $\frac{2}{2}$ time (alla breve)__

    d) Name and explain the sign at the letter B. __tie - hold for the combined value__

    e) Identify the number of complete measures played in the music (observe the repeat sign). __16__

    f) Circle if the Gavotte tempo should be played: *molto presto* or (*tempo di gavotta*)

    g) Circle if the meter (indicated by the scoops in measure 1) is: (duple) or triple or quadruple.

Go to **GSGMUSIC.com** - For Easy Access to listening to Bach's French Suite No. 5 in G Major.

# MUSIC APPRECIATION - FRENCH SUITE No. 5 in G MAJOR, BWV 816 GIGUE by J.S. BACH

The Gigue is the last piece from the French Suite No. 5 in G Major, BWV 816 by J.S. Bach. The Gigue has several melodic lines combined into a multi-voiced texture called polyphonic (poly means two or more).

> Polyphonic means two or more independent melodic lines, also called voices. Each melodic line (voice) is indicated by the stem direction. When only one melodic line is present, normal stem direction rules apply.
>
> The first upper melodic line is indicated by all stems up. The second melodic line is indicated by all stems down (on the same staff). The third melodic line is indicated on the lower staff with normal stem direction rules. When more than one melodic line is indicated on the same staff, rests are placed off the staff.
>
> In 12/16 time, each measure contains the value of 12 sixteenth notes. The sixteenth notes are divided into 4 equal groups of 3 sixteenth notes, creating quadruple meter.

Gigue from the French Suite No. 5 in G Major, BWV 816 — J.S. Bach

1. Analyze the music by answering the questions below.

   a) Circle if each melodic line begins on: (an upbeat) or a downbeat.

   b) How many melodic lines are played in:  mm. 1 to 3  _1_ ;  mm. 4 to 6  _2_ ;  mm. 7 to 9  _3_ .

   c) Circle if the meter (indicated by the scoops in measure 1) is:  duple  or  triple  or  (quadruple.)

# Ultimate Music Theory
## Level 3 Theory Exam

Total Score: ___ / 100

The Ultimate Music Theory™ Rudiments Workbooks, Supplemental Workbooks and Exams prepare students for successful completion of the Royal Conservatory of Music Theory Levels.

1. a) Write the enharmonic equivalent for each of the following notes. Use whole notes.
   b) Name the notes.

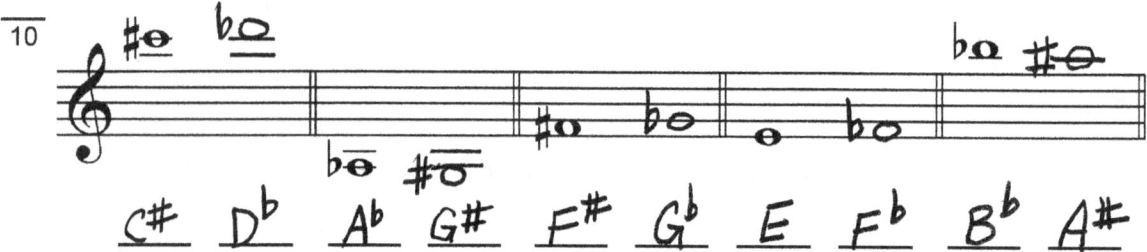

C#  Db  Ab  G#  F#  Gb  E  Fb  Bb  A#

2. a) Name the Major key.
   b) Transpose the melody down one octave in the Treble Clef.

Key: Bb Major

c) Name the minor key.
d) Transpose the melody up one octave in the Bass Clef.

Key: e minor

UltimateMusicTheory.com © Copyright 2017 Gloryland Publishing. All Rights Reserved.

# Ultimate Music Theory
## Level 3 Theory Exam

3. a) Add one rest below each bracket to complete each measure.

b) Add the correct Time Signature below each bracket.

c) Add the missing bar lines.

4. a) Write the following harmonic intervals above each given note. Use whole notes. Use accidentals when necessary.

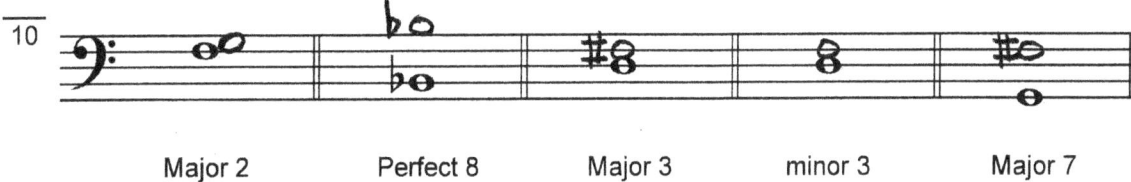

    Major 2        Perfect 8       Major 3       minor 3       Major 7

b) Name the following melodic intervals.

    Maj 6      min 3      Per 4      Per 5      Maj 3

# Ultimate Music Theory
## Level 3 Theory Exam

5.  a) Name the Key.
    b) Write the Functional Chord Symbol below each triad.
    c) Write the Root/Quality Chord Symbol above each triad

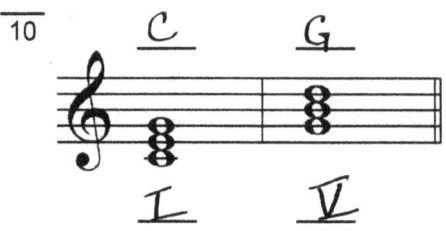

Major key: C Major

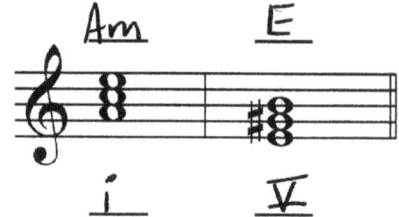

Relative minor key: a minor

Major key: G Major

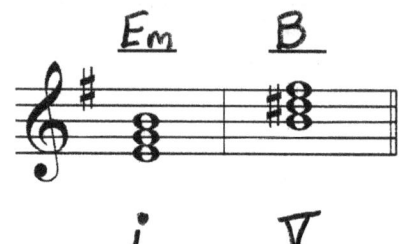

Relative minor key: e minor

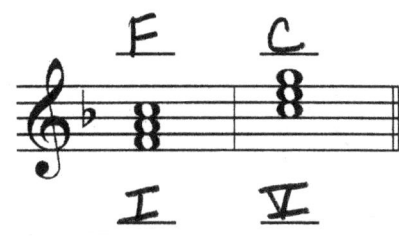

Major key: F Major

Relative minor key: d minor

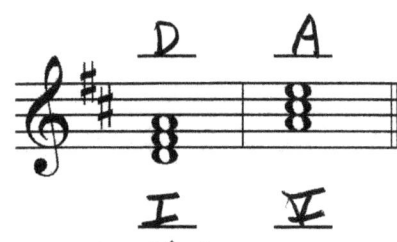

Major key: D Major

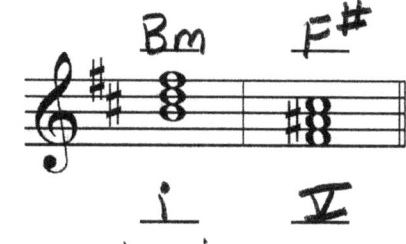

Relative minor key: b minor

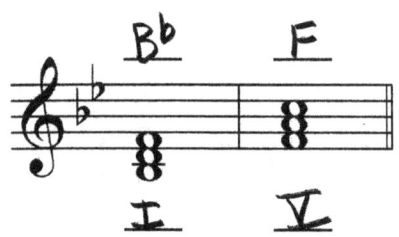

Major key: B♭ Major

Relative minor key: g minor

# Ultimate Music Theory
## Level 3 Theory Exam

6. Write the following scales, ascending and descending. Use a Key Signature and any necessary accidentals. Use whole notes.

10  a) g minor harmonic scale in the Bass Clef.

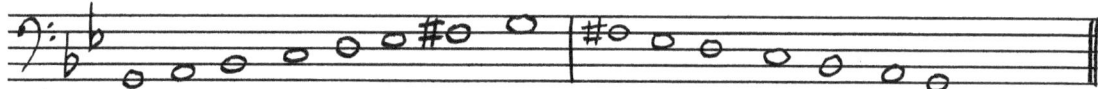

b) B flat Major scale in the Treble Clef.

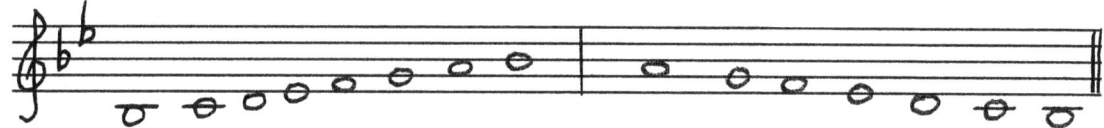

c) b minor melodic scale in the Bass Clef.

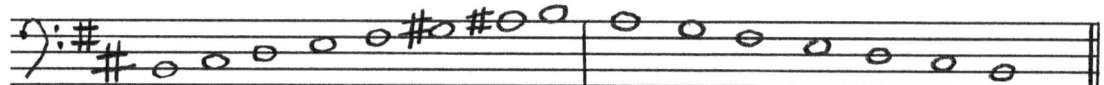

d) d minor natural scale in the Treble Clef.

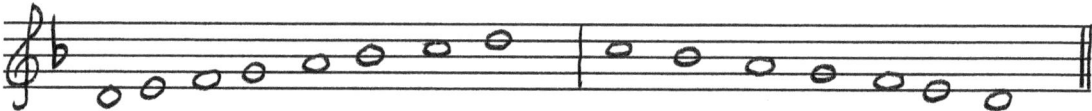

e) D Major scale in the Bass Clef.

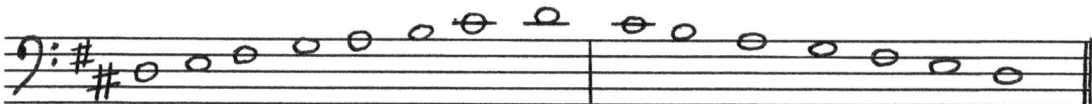

7. a) Name the minor key.
   b) Write the Scale Degree Name of each note below the staff.

10

Key:    a minor    g minor    e minor    d minor    b minor
Degree: Tonic      Dominant   Subdominant  Leading Tone  Subtonic

# Ultimate Music Theory
## Level 3 Theory Exam

8. Indicate whether the definition of each Musical Term or Sign is True (T) or False (F).

___/10

| Music Term or Sign | Definition | True (T) or False (F) |
|---|---|---|
| a) *marcato* | marked or stressed | Example: __T__ |
| b) *cantabile* | sweet, graceful | __F__ |
| c) *dal segno, D.S.* | from the sign | __T__ |
| d) $8^{va}$ | interval of an octave | __T__ |
| e) *maestoso* | majestic | __T__ |
| f) $8^{va}$- - - - - ⌐ | play one octave above the written pitch | __F__ |

9. Complete the following history questions by filling in the blanks.

___/10

a) J.S. Bach was a composer who wrote music in the era called __Baroque__.

b) Bach gave his wife a notebook of music called the __Anna Magdalena Notebook__

c) A popular Baroque keyboard instrument with 4 - 6 octaves was the __harpsichord__.

d) An upbeat or pickup beat is called an __anacrusis__.

e) Name three Baroque Dances - __Menuet__, __Gavotte__ and __Gigue__.

f) Name the composer of the Menuet in G Major, BWV Anh. 114. __Christian Petzold__

g) Name the composer of the French Suite No. 5 in G Major, BWV 817. __J.S. Bach__

h) The texture of two or more independent melodic lines is called __polyphonic texture__

i) Harpsichord music often featured embellishment symbols called __trills (mordent)__.

j) Baroque dynamics that alter from loud to soft are called __terraced dynamics__.

# Ultimate Music Theory
## Level 3 Theory Exam

10. Analyze the following piece of music by answering the questions below.

*Menuet in G Minor, BWV Anh. 115*

From the *Notebook for Anna Magdalena Bach*

a) Circle if the "Menuet" is:   a Graceful German Dance   or   (a Formal French Dance.)

b) Add the measure number in the box at the beginning of lines 2 and 3.

c) Identify the letter names of the notes at the letter A.   __Bb__   __A__   __G__

d) Circle if the melodic motive pattern at the letter B and the letter C is:   (similar)   or   different.

e) Identify the interval at the letter D.   __min 3__   Circle if this interval is:   melodic   or   (harmonic.)

f) Identify the interval at the letter E.   __Per 4__   Circle if this interval is:   (melodic)   or   harmonic.

g) Circle if the melody at the letter F is:   stepping up   or   (stepping down)   or   repeating.

h) Circle if the ornamentation sign at the letter G is:   (a mordent)   or   an appoggiatura   or   a trill.

i) For the triad at the letter H, identify the Root note.   __F__   Identify the Quality.   __Major__

j) Identify the number of measures written.   __16__   Identify the number of measures played.   __32__

Bonus - Play "Menuet in G Minor" on your instrument.

# Ultimate Music Theory Certificate

_____

*has successfully completed all the requirements of the*

# Music Theory Level 3

_____  _____
*Music Teacher*                                       *Date*

Enriching Lives Through Music Education

www.ingramcontent.com/pod-product-compliance
Lightning Source LLC
Chambersburg PA
CBHW081733100526
44591CB00016B/2598